With love
to Alex &
his 'top guns'
for christmas &
2013

all our love,
mum d dad

D0585259

THE
LITTLE
BOOK
OF
BOXING

GRAEME KENT

First published 2009

Reprinted 2012

The History Press
The Mill, Brimscombe Port
Stroud, Gloucestershire, GL5 2QG
www.thehistorypress.co.uk

British Library Cataloguing in Publication Data.
A catalogue record for this book is available from the British Library.

ISBN 978 0 7524 5253 1

Typesetting and origination by The History Press
Printed in Great Britain

THE AUTHOR

Graeme Kent has written fourteen novels, over a hundred non-fiction books, prize-winning stage and television plays and hundreds of radio scripts. His books have been published in over 20 different countries. He has been a BBC producer and as a freelance journalist he has written for many national newspapers and magazines. His boxing history book *The Great White Hopes* was short-listed for the William Hill Sports Book of the Year award.

INTRODUCTION

The first professional boxer I ever saw in the ring was a Canadian lightweight called Danny Webb. My father took me to see him box an exhibition bout at a small hall in Portsmouth towards the end of the Second World War. I was thrilled by the ambience of it all, the clang of the bell, the rattle of buckets in the corner, the shuffle of feet on canvas, the slap of the gloves and the stentorian, rhythmic breathing of the contestants. I also heard the first of thousands of boxing clichés, too many of which I was later to use professionally, when Webb's opponent trudged back to his corner at the end of a torrid round and muttered disconsolately through swollen lips, 'He's boxing clever!'

My next contact with the ring occurred several years later when Bob Parkin's boxing booth started to visit Southsea Common every summer. It was little more than a tent, with a false front and a startlingly unrealistic painting on a wooden board of Joe Louis fighting Tommy Farr, flapping in the wind above a stage on which the fighters paraded.

Although it was 60 years ago, I can still remember vividly the boxers on that platform. Pat Mulcahy, introduced as the middleweight, light heavyweight and heavyweight champion of Ireland; Len Davies, a battle-scarred Welsh featherweight; Berry Reed, a Jamaican middleweight, and Sam Johnson, a hulking black heavyweight.

Admittance to the booth was two shillings with a sometimes-affordable half-price for children. Members of the crowd were invited to try to last six rounds with the booth fighter for a prize of five pounds. My father was bringing up a family on just about half of this amount in 1948, so it was a fair offer to recently demobilised young hopefuls looking for work.

The fights and fighters varied in intensity. Mulcahy, resplendent in mauve trunks, was smooth and economical, ducking, slipping, with a tolerant, seen-it-all smile, sliding easily along the ropes. In the final rounds, however, he would change from an affable Dr Jekyll to a clinical Mr Hyde, usually producing a stunning unexpected knockout punch to end the contest.

Davies was altogether sadder and grittier; you suspected that he had secret sorrows. He first introduced me to the concept that some of the booth bouts must have been arranged so that the novice challenger could last long enough to make a fight of it for the patrons. One night, a contender got through with a lucky punch and opened a cut among the network of tired scar tissue above the Welshman's eye. The blow had a startling effect. Not only had Davies been hurt, he probably realised that the injury would mean a couple of weeks off work and a resultant loss of wages. He dabbed at the cut with the thumb of his glove and then before he could prevent himself, he stopped coasting and rammed two violent hooks on to the jaw of his opponent, sending the unfortunate man reeling across the ring.

Paradoxically, the crowd hooted at the example of the savagery they had paid to see. Davies, who was plainly a decent man, regretted his action at once. He shuffled across the ring sheepishly and held his challenger up until the bell rang.

In addition, the booth personnel always had to know how to work their audiences. When Sam Johnson found himself up against a much younger and stronger challenger, he disposed of his opponent by sidestepping a rush and nudging the hapless youth clear out of the ring with a quick but powerful shrug of his shoulder into the passing boy's back. Bob Parkin who was refereeing the bout completed the count quickly, before the other man could climb back into the ring.

There were angry jeers from the crowd. Parkin took in the situation and faced the incensed mob benevolently, like a popular headmaster who had experienced most of the vicissitudes that life had to offer at the hands of unruly pupils. 'Ah,' he explained to us tolerantly, 'there aren't many tricks that Sam doesn't know.' The words, complicitly inviting the crowd to join his world of masculine duplicity, had their desired effect. The crowd roared with laughter, forgot the harshly treated challenger, and threw coins into the ring – the traditional 'nobbins' to be shared by both fighters.

Since those early days I have been hooked on boxing, first as an undistinguished practitioner, then as referee, second, trainer, radio commentator and writer. I would like to dedicate this book to the thousands of fighters over the years who have been kind enough to share their skills, time and memories with me. It would be impossible to mention all these warriors of the working day, but among those I remember with particular affection through the mists of time are Billy Pleace, journeyman and gentleman, who had his moment of glory when, so bravely, he took British bantamweight champion Johnny King the ten-rounds distance; Johnny Smith, ABA light heavyweight semi-finalist and solid pro, who had one of the most beautiful boxing styles I have ever seen on a big man; Danny O'Sullivan, British and European champion and charming raconteur; amateur heavyweight Les Peach, ring opponent of Ugandan dictator Idi Amin, and Vernon Scannell, booth fighter and coruscating writer, whose poem 'Peerless Jim Driscoll' should be a set text for every examination board. I would like to thank Zoe O'Brien of the British Boxing Board of Control for her help with statistics.

I am deeply indebted, also, to Michelle Tilling, my editor at the History Press, for asking me to write this book and for providing such sympathetic guidance throughout. The work would certainly never have been completed without the tactful encouragement and unfailing expertise of my superb agent Isabel White. I am truly fortunate to have had both of them in my corner.

The Marquess of Queensberry Rules

The Marquess of Queensberry Rules, which brought boxing into the modern era, were not devised by the Marquess. They were the brainchild of a newspaper writer and former amateur boxer and oarsman, John Graham Chambers (1843–83). They were formulated in 1867 and revolutionised the sport. They introduced the use of gloves and stipulated three-minute rounds, with a minute's rest between rounds, and a ten-second count to decide a knockout. John Sholto Douglas, the eighth Marquess of Queensberry, a keen follower of boxing, allowed his name to be used for the rules, which remained in force until 1929, when they were updated. The Marquess went on to achieve notoriety when he hounded the playwright Oscar Wilde after the latter had conducted a homosexual affair with Queensberry's son, Lord Alfred Douglas. Wilde sued Queensberry for libel, eventually lost, and was sentenced to two years' hard labour.

Chambers, the real architect of the Queensberry Rules, also helped to organise the Boat Race and the first FA Cup Final and was the champion road-walker of England.

The Booths

From the first days of boxing, the sport was brought to remote areas by travelling booths. These provided exhibition contests and challenges from the booth fighters to all-comers. George Taylor, a travelling showman who claimed the bare-knuckle title in 1735, was the first title-holder to tour in this manner. Since then many future champions learned their trade in the booths. Fighters like Jimmy Wilde and Freddie Mills served their apprenticeships with itinerant fairs.

Life on the booths was hard. Up to 20 shows a day were scheduled. One fighter, middleweight Len Johnson, once fought on every performance for three days, a total of 60 bouts. In the late 1950s, the British Boxing Board of Control banned licensed boxers from working on the booths, hastening their closure. Most of the travelling booths finally came to an end in the 1960s and 1970s.

ATTENDANCES

Some of the first bare-knuckle contests attracted crowds of only a few hundred patrons. By the end of the twentieth century, however, boxing was an extremely big business, attracting vast crowds and television audiences in the millions. The largest recorded paying crowd at an outdoor competition occurred on 20 February 1993 at the Estadio Azteca football stadium in Mexico City. There were five world title fights on the bill that night. Between 130,000 and 136,000 people paid to watch the undefeated champion Julio César Chávez fight American Greg Haugen in a WBC light welterweight title match. There had been ill-feeling between the two since they had fallen out during a Las Vegas sparring session several years earlier. Haugen, the official number two contender, said disparagingly of the champion's undefeated record after more than 80 contests, '60 of the guys he fought were just Tijuana cabdrivers.' Chávez stopped Haugen in five rounds and then informed his beaten opponent, 'Now you see I don't fight with taxi drivers.'

DODGY PROMOTERS

A promoter's lot is not an easy one. Many have lost their shirts on over-ambitious tournaments. In 1914, New York lightweight Jack Bernstein was signed up for a contest promoted by a local butcher. The evening was a total disaster and the butcher lost everything. He had to pay his fighters off in kind. As a bottom-of-the-bill fighter, Bernstein received half a salami for his efforts.

THE GREAT CHAMPIONS:
1 – JIMMY WILDE: 1892–1969

Main weight: flyweight
Contests: 152 **Won:** 137 (KO: 99) **Lost:** 5 **Drew:** 2
Variously known as 'the Ghost with a Hammer in his Hand' and 'the Mighty Atom', the scrawny and emaciated Jimmy Wilde always weighed-in considerably below the flyweight limit and gave away weight in most of his contests. He never scaled more than 8 stone in weight and was usually far lighter. Nevertheless, in addition to being fast and elusive, he possessed an incredibly heavy punch in either hand and won most of his bouts on knockouts. He was born in Merthyr Tydfil and then moved to Tylorstown, Mid-Glamorgan. Like most of his contemporaries he started down the mines, but by 16 he was taking on all-comers in a travelling boxing booth. At first he was regarded as a physical freak, but, after remaining undefeated in his first 101 fights, his boxing skills made him a headliner. In 1910 he left the booths under the tutelage of a shrewd manager, Ted Lewis. Lewis saw to it that whenever possible Wilde's opponents had to reduce their weight and come in at a weakened state.

In 1914 Wilde took the European title from Frenchman Eugene Husson. He then claimed the world title when he stopped the Young Zulu Kid.

He was stopped in an upset decision by the Scottish fighter Tancy Lee in 11 rounds, but won the return contest. After his seconds had thrown in the towel after the first encounter with Lee, Wilde ordered them never to do so again, no matter how badly he might be getting beaten.

He defeated Joe Conn in 12 rounds in 1918 and after a dispute over the purse, the promoter gave his wife £3,000-worth of diamonds. After serving as a Physical Training Instructor in the First World War, Wilde defeated a number of highly rated American fighters, although he was stopped by former world bantamweight champion Pete Herman, giving away a great deal of weight in the process.

In his last fight in the ring he was knocked out by Pancho Villa in 7 rounds at the New York Polo Grounds. He retired to write a newspaper column, where his system for predicting winners was 'You can't close your eyes to the fact that it's always the wallop that wins.'

When he was an old man in 1960, he was set upon by a thug at Cardiff railway station and badly beaten. He never really recovered. He spent his last days in a nursing home and died in 1969.

COLLEGE BOYS: 1 – SIR WILFRED THESIGER

Boxing has tended to be a working-class sport, but a number of undergraduates and graduates have taken it up with varying degrees of success. Sir Wilfred Thesiger (1910–2003) was one of the last of the great explorers, travelling through the notorious Empty Quarter of the southern region of the Arabian peninsula and the marshlands of southern Iraq, as well as parts of Iran, Africa and Pakistan. He wrote best-selling books about his exploits and won the DSO in the Second World War. He boxed for Oxford University as a light heavyweight from 1930 for three years, becoming captain of the team in the last year.

An aesthetic loner, Thesiger was guarded about his sexuality. When someone once asked him if he was gay, the explorer floored him with a single punch.

Vote for Pinky!

In 1922, Mike Collins, editor of the Minneapolis weekly *Boxing Blade,* decided that there was too much of a gap between the lightweight limit of 135lb and the welterweight maximum of 147lb. He set out to establish a new weight class half-way between, with a top weight of 140lb. He called it the junior welterweight division and asked his readers to write in with suggestions for the first champion in this weight class. A Milwaukee fighter called Pinky Mitchell received the most votes and was declared by Collins to be the new division's first champion, thus adding a whole new meaning to the term 'newspaper decision'.

Post-Match Comments

'Hey, Ma, your bad boy did it!'
*A delighted Rocky Graziano, a former juvenile delinquent,
in a radio interview after taking the world middleweight
title from Tony Zale.*

'What happened?'
>   *Dave 'Boy' Green upon recovering consciousness after being knocked out by Sugar Ray Leonard in Landover, Maryland, in 1980.*

'I got too goddamned careless!'
>   *Tami Mauriello explaining his one-round knockout loss to world heavyweight champion Joe Louis at Yankee Stadium in 1946. The broadcasting authorities were so shocked by the use of the expletive that they took the interview off the air and returned to the studio.*

'Ask me how I feel. Go on, ask me how I feel.'
'How do you feel, Terry?'
'Exotic!'
>   *Terry Marsh interviewed in the ring after winning the vacant European light welterweight title from Alessandro Scapecchi at Monte Carlo in 1985.*

'Honey, I forgot to duck!'
>   *Former heavyweight champion Jack Dempsey explaining his battered face and title loss to Gene Tunney to his wife Estelle in Philadelphia in 1926.*

'I am too young. I should have known better. But I will beat him yet.'
>   *The Michigan Chick after losing a 67-round contest in Montana in 1868.*

'I have $100,000 and a farm in Kansas!'
>   *Mantra muttered continuously by a shell-shocked Jess Willard after his third round stoppage loss to Jack Dempsey at Toledo in 1919.*

'Was it a good fight?'
> *The first question James J. Braddock asked when he came round after being knocked out by Joe Louis in Chicago in 1937.*

'I have no excuse to offer. I was beaten. I was in fine condition, but never boxed more miserably. After the fifth round I could do nothing with my right. I do not know what was wrong. It simply would not work. Wade is certainly a clever and hard boxer. He deserves credit and I give it to him.'
> *Kid Oglesby after losing his Montana lightweight championship to Jack Wade in Butte, Montana, 1901.*

'From now on match me with one fighter at a time!'
> *Middleweight Harry Greb to his manager after he had been outsmarted by the fast Mike Gibbons, 'the St Paul Phantom', in 1919.*

'Nobody ever lived as strong as this guy!'
> *Jack Britton after fighting Benny Leonard in 1918.*

'Lead me out there; I want to shake his hand.'
> *A half-blinded Jack Dempsey to his corner men after losing his first fight to Gene Tunney in 1926.*

'I have fought once too often.'
> *John L. Sullivan addresses crowd after losing to James J. Corbett.*

An Actor's Life for Me! 1 – Canada Lee

Many fighters have enjoyed using their fighting fame to become actors. Sports writer Bob Edgren pointed this out in 1923, 'All fighters, just after winning the title, like to take a little rest and accumulate the soft currency for a little while. Some of them grow so fond of the footlights that they talk about being natural-born actors, and tell the world how sorry they are they ever took up anything so crude as fighting for a living when they had unsuspected talent for better things.'

Canada Lee was a leading welterweight who lost to ex-champion Jack Britton during a career that encompassed 77 fights in the 1920s and '30s. Forced to abandon the sport when he suffered a detached retina in one eye during a bout, he drifted into acting, becoming a member of Orson Welles' celebrated stage company and appearing on Broadway in the lead in Richard Wright's *Native Son*. Opportunities for black actors were limited in the 1930s, but Lee scored in Alfred Hitchcock's film *Lifeboat*. His most famous role was that of the former champion who befriended and trained John Garfield in *Body and Soul*. Lee's acting career came to an end when he was denounced as a Communist sympathiser in Senator McCarthy's notorious witch hunts of the 1950s. Lee died in 1952. His friend, fellow actor Ossie Davis said, 'Lee couldn't find a job anywhere and died of a broken heart.'

Fixed?

Over the years questions have been raised over the probity of some major fights. As Jake LaMotta, who admitted to losing a bout deliberately, sighed, 'You win some, you throw some!'

On 31 August 1900, the former world heavyweight champion James J. 'Gentleman Jim' Corbett was scheduled to meet a wily character known as Kid McCoy, whose real name was Norman Selby. For some time before the bout, rumours had been circulating that the result had been fixed in advance. All the same, 8,000 spectators turned up at Madison Square Garden to see what was scheduled as New York's last professional boxing match before the sport was to be banned in the city by politicians.

The contest, a 'no decision' one, proved to be very dull, reinforcing the rumours. To add fuel to the fire, the wives of both Corbett and McCoy, who were having marital problems with their respective spouses, agreed that the contest had been 'fixed'. Both fighters denied the charge, but one prominent New York newspaper published a banner headline announcing 'McCoy Fight Fixed'.

In 1948, a rated American heavyweight called Lee Oma was knocked out in the fourth round by the British heavyweight champion Bruce Woodcock. Oma, a noted playboy and drinker who had been paid $100,000 for his lack of effort, made few attempts to hit his opponent and succumbed to the first hard punch the British champion threw. As Oma lay in a crumpled heap on the canvas, the irate crowd chanted 'Lie down! Lie down!' to the tune of 'Bow Bells'. A headline in the *Daily Mirror* said simply 'Oma! Aroma! Coma!' Promoter Jack Solomons denied that there had been anything underhand about the bout but admitted that the evening had been 'a fiasco.'

In 1951, smart-boxing Billy Graham lost a controversial split decision to Kid Gavilán for the world welterweight title. There were rumours that mobster Frank Carbo had been involved in arranging the result. Before the fight he had approached Graham's manager and told him that Graham could have the title if Carbo was cut in for 20 per cent of his future earnings. Years later, one of the judges for the match summoned Billy Graham's manager to his hospital deathbed and confessed that he had been ordered to cast his vote for Gavilán, no matter how well Graham fought.

ON THE RUN

Several boxing champions who showed great courage in the ring did not display the same amount of fortitude when it came to serving their countries during the war. At least two of them deserted.

Freddie Mills had been a promising young West Country boxer when he had been conscripted into the RAF. He was made a physical training instructor and was allowed to continue with his boxing career. In 1942, at the age of 22, he fought a fellow serviceman, Pilot Officer Len Harvey for the latter's British light heavyweight title and knocked his superior officer out.

It should have been a good time for Mills but he found that he could not cope with his RAF duties, his boxing career and his new-found fame. Only a few days after beating Harvey, the new champion deserted from his unit. He hitchhiked to London and spent an aimless week as a tourist, visiting St Paul's Cathedral and the Tower of London. Then he went back to his unit and gave himself up.

At first it looked as if Mills would face a court-martial. However, a decision was made at the highest levels in the Air Ministry that such bad publicity would not reflect well on the RAF. Instead, Mills was sent hastily to India, where he spent the rest of the war fighting exhibitions for troops.

After the war Mills resumed his fighting career. He won the world light heavyweight championship at his second attempt and retired with a record of only 17 defeats in 97 bouts. He appeared in films and on television and opened a nightclub. He died by his own hand in 1965.

In the USA, Rocky Graziano (Rocco Barbella) was a street hoodlum who had served terms in reformatories and prison before he was drafted into the US Army. On his first full day in the service, Graziano floored a corporal and an officer and deserted. He kept alive by boxing until the military police caught up with him. During this period he took part in seven contests, including one in front of a crowd of 2,000 soldiers. Graziano was court-martialled, dishonourably discharged and sent to a military prison for a year. He became a star of the inmates' boxing team. In 1943 he resumed his boxing career and soon made a name for himself. He took part in three thrilling contests with the world middleweight champion Tony Zale, winning one of them and thus briefly becoming the champion.

When he retired from the ring he had engaged in 83 contests, winning 67 of them, with 52 knockouts. He became a television personality and after-dinner speaker and lent his name to a best-selling ghosted autobiography, *Somebody Up There Likes Me*. Rocky Graziano died in 1990.

A Champion's Lament

'My first five wives were all good housekeepers. Each one of them kept the house after they left.'

Willie Pep, World Featherweight Champion.

FIGHT FILMS – THE BEST:
1 – *BODY AND SOUL* (1947)

Director: Robert Rossen **Screenplay:** Abraham Polonsky
Leading Players: John Garfield, Lili Palmer, Anne Revere,
William Conrad, Canada Lee

A young boxer (Garfield) fights his way out of poverty
to become a champion in order to support his widowed
mother. In the process he develops a liking for the high life
and alienates his mother (Revere), fiancée (Palmer) and
trainer (Lee). When the last-named dies as a result of the
ring punishment he has taken, the boxer tries to shake off
his mob connections. He rejects his crooked associates and
wins a fight he has been scheduled to throw. A clichéd script
is redeemed by fine, atmospheric direction and some of the
best and most realistic fight scenes ever put on celluloid.

The strength of this movie lies in its photography by the
great James Wong Howe, who filmed the climactic fight
and captures its ferocious fluidity by circling the boxers
on roller skates. Garfield and Rossen studied thousands of
real bouts to get the effect they needed. There is a terrific,
Oscar-nominated, performance from Garfield as the bitter
kid from the wrong side of the tracks who finally becomes
a man.

MANAGERS AND TRAINERS ON FIGHTERS

'I'm going to take an extra stool into the ring. One is for
Vinny to sit on and the other is for me to throw at him if he
doesn't listen to me!'
    *Manager Lou Duva on his plan of action for his less than
attentive middleweight Vinny Pazienza.*

'If you don't want to fight this guy, I will!'
Teddy Atlas, annoyed at his fighter Michael Moorer's lack of action against champion Evander Holyfield, was sitting on the boxer's stool when Moorer returned to his corner after one particularly lacklustre round. His scorn had the desired effect. Moorer increased his effort and won the title.

'Liston has a lot of good qualities. It's his bad qualities that are not so good.'
Manager George Katz, manager, on world heavyweight champion Sonny Liston.

'His dressing room looked like a Spice Girls convention'.
A member of British middleweight champion Ryan Rhodes' training staff describes the convivial dressing room atmosphere before one of the boxer's bouts.

'Get up, you unnatural son of a bitch! Have you no regard for my feelings?'
Manager Willus Britt to his brother and lightweight fighter Jimmy, after the latter had been knocked down.

'He was the perfect combination – showman, fighter and rat.'
Manager Jackie McCoy, manager, on fighter Art Aragon.

'Sit down, son. It's all over. But nobody will ever forget what you did here today.'
A compassionate trainer, Eddie Futch, pulls an exhausted Joe Frazier out of his 1975 Manila fight with Muhammad Ali at the end of the 14th round.

Fighters on Managers and Trainers

'Never in the field of human conflict have so few taken so much from so many.'

Saoul Mamby's opinion of managers.

'Everybody wants a piece of the cake, but my cake has no slices.'

World heavyweight champion Ingemar Johansson's explanation as to why he disliked hangers-on.

'I'm just a prawn in this game!'

Morose heavyweight Brian London ruminates on boxing politics.

'All I know about managers is that when the bell rings to start a fight, I go into the ring and they go out of it.'

World heavyweight title contender Buster Mathis.

'I got robbed by the king of robbers. If I had to get robbed, I'm glad it was by the best man in the country at robbing.'

Jess Willard on Doc Kearns, manager of his victor, Jack Dempsey. Kearns was accused of wrapping his fighter's hands in plaster of Paris before Dempsey's victory at Toledo in 1919.

'If you've got a dollar he wants the first 26 cents.'

Tex Cobb on manager and promoter Don King.

'For twelve years my lips were surgically attached to his ass.'

Larry Holmes on Don King.

'They cut him four ways – up, down, deep and often.'
Heavyweight Mike DeJohn on Sonny Liston's relationship
with his managers.

'That's it! The free rides are over. Get out and walk, all of you!'
Light heavyweight champion Willie Pastrano to his corner
men as he was getting trounced by Terry Downs for his
title at Manchester in 1964. Fortunately, Pastrano rallied
and defeated Downs in the 11th round and thus ensured
continuity of employment for his manager and trainer.

What advice do my seconds give me? They tell me that once
I climb between those ropes I'm on my own.'
Marvin Hagler.

'They say what a smart fighter I was. I couldn't have been.
I had a manager for two years who fed me nothing but
doughnuts and black coffee – and had me loving it!'
Willie Pep, world featherweight champion.

'Nurse me, nurse me and I'll whip him yet!'
Bare-knuckle fighter Thomas McCoy begs his seconds after
he has been knocked down 40 times against Christopher
Lilly in 1842. He went out for one more round and was
knocked out, never to recover consciousness.

FOUL! 1 – GOLOTA AND BOWE

Boxing laws have been applied with increasing stringency
over the years but there have always been boxers who have
sought ways to circumnavigate the rules and referees who
have been determined to apply them.

Heavyweight Riddick Bowe always knew how to wind up his Polish opponent Andrew Golota, 1988 Olympic bronze medallist and Warsaw street fighter. Golota left for the USA to avoid facing charges of assault and robbery at a disco in his home city. He ran up a good boxing record in his adopted homeland and in 1996 was matched with a leading contender, Riddick Bowe. For most of the fight the Pole was well on top, causing the American all sorts of trouble. In the 7th round, however, Bowe hit his opponent with an illegal rabbit punch. Always quick to take offence, Golota responded with a terrific blow below the belt, dropping his adversary. The referee disqualified Golota. The crowd poured into the ring and a mini-riot ensued. Golota was struck by a mobile phone and his trainer Lou Duva suffered a heart attack. A few months later the fighters were rematched in what one writer called 'a back alley brawl'. Again Golota was well on top, knocking his opponent down twice, but again he lost his head. In the ninth round he hit Bowe below the belt again. Once more he was disqualified. Before the bout Golota had announced, a trifle optimistically, 'I expect a clean, fair fight.'

Weight Divisions

In the 1920s, the National Sporting Club established eight weight divisions at which boxers could compete. They were:

Flyweight:	8 stone and under
Bantamweight:	8 stone 6lb and under
Featherweight:	9 stone and under
Lightweight:	9 stone 9lb and under
Welterweight:	10 stone 7lb and under

Middleweight: 11 stone 6lb and under
Light-heavyweight: 12 stone 7lb and under
Heavyweight: any weight

Today there are 17 weight divisions in professional boxing. There are many disputes about the first champions in some of the first weight divisions.

Mini Flyweight (Strawweight)
Top weight limit: 105lb. Established: 1987.
First champion: Kyung-Yung Lee, South Korea.

Light Flyweight
Top weight limit: 108lb. Established: 1975.
First champion: Franco Udella, Italy.

Flyweight
Top weight limit: 112lb. Established: 1909.
First champion: Sid Smith, England.

Super Flyweight
Top weight limit: 115lb. Established: 1980.
First champion: Rafael Orono, Venezuela.

Bantamweight
Top weight limit: 118lb. Established: 1888.
First champion: George Dixon, USA.

Super Bantamweight
Top weight limit: 122lb. Established: 1976.
First champion: Rigoberto Riasco, Panama.

Featherweight
Top weight limit: 126lb. Established: 1890.
First champion: Billy Murphy, Australia

Junior Lightweight
Top weight limit: 130lb. Established: 1921.
First champion: Johnny Dundee, USA.

Lightweight
Top weight limit: 135lb. Established: 1847.
First champion: Arthur Chambers (bare-knuckle), Britain.

Junior Welterweight
Top weight limit: 140lb. Established: 1922.
First champion: Pinky Mitchell, USA.

Welterweight
Top weight limit: 147lb. Established: 1888.
First champion: Paddy Duffy, USA.

Junior Middleweight
Top weight limit: 154lb. Established: 1962.
First champion: Denny Moyer, USA.

Middleweight
Top weight limit: 160lb. Established: 1884.
First champion: Jack (Nonpareil) Dempsey, USA.

Super Middleweight
Top weight limit: 168lb. Established: 1984.
First champion: Murray Sutherland, Scotland.

Light Heavyweight
Top weight limit: 175lb. Established: 1903.
First champion: Jack Root, USA.

Cruiserweight
Top weight limit: 190lb. Established: 1979.
First champion: Marvin Camel, USA.

Heavyweight
Top weight limit: None. Established: 1892.
 First champion (gloves): James J.Corbett, USA.

NEXT!

A number of fighters have had more than one fight in an evening in order to pad out the bill. English heavyweight Phil Scott, however, almost made a habit of it. In December 1926, he defeated Armando De Carolis on a disqualification in four rounds and knocked out Leon Sebilo in two. In the following year, at Premierland in Stepney, on the same evening he knocked out Helmut Siewert in three rounds and Harry Reeve, also in three rounds.

This effort paled into insignificance compared with the feat of George Foreman. In 1975, still smarting from losing his heavyweight crown to Muhammad Ali in Zaire, Foreman defeated five opponents in the same evening in Toronto.

Pride of place, however, goes to Bob Fitzsimmons. One evening at the World's Fair in Chicago in 1893 he took on seven opponents. Fitzsimmons, who was the middleweight champion of the world at the time, promised $40 to any man who could last six rounds with him, while he was to receive a purse if he knocked out all seven. In all he fought a total of 19 rounds that evening, but knocked out every opponent.

THE GREAT CHAMPIONS:
2 – STANLEY KETCHEL: 1886–1910

Main weight: middleweight **Contests:** 64 **Won:** 53 (KO: 48) **Lost:** 5 **Drew:** 5

Known as 'the Michigan Assassin' and 'The Fighting Hobo', Ketchel was the most aggressive all-action fighter of his time, with an enormous following of supporters.

Both his parents were murdered while he was a child. He ran away from what was left of his home to ride the rails and live and fight in hobo camps. Slowly he moved further west until he settled in Butte, Montana. At the age of 16 he beat up a bouncer in a bar dispute and was offered the man's job. He did his job so efficiently that he started getting offers to fight professionally. He moonlighted by taking on challengers at a local boxing booth for $20 a week. He attracted attention when he performed well against Tommy Ryan, the world middleweight champion who was on a whistle-stop tour of the West.

The handsome Ketchel never took a backward step in any of his contests. He knew that he owed his success to his hard hitting, saying, 'If a fighter hasn't got a punch, he might as well quit the ring. There's a lot of scienced boys eating snowballs this winter.'

In his first four years as a professional he scored 35 wins inside the distance, against two defeats. He took the vacant world middleweight title from Jack 'Twin' Sullivan and made six defences of the championship. With his new-found wealth he embarked upon a hedonistic lifestyle and started neglecting his training.

In 1909, he gave away over 40lb in weight and challenged Jack Johnson for the latter's heavyweight championship. The two men made a secret pact that Johnson would go easy on his opponent for the sake of the revenue from motion picture rights. In the 12th round, Ketchel tried to pull a fast one, stepping in and knocking the unsuspecting Johnson down. Unfortunately Johnson got up, extremely irate. He hit Ketchel so hard that some of the middleweight's teeth were later found embedded in Johnson's glove. It was almost the end of the road for Stan Ketchel. High living, excesses and too many brutal toe-to-toe battles had taken their toll on the still-young man. He found it increasingly difficult to defeat opponents he would once have beaten with ease. He continued to chase after women, and this was to bring about his ultimate downfall. He went to a farm near Conway, Missouri, in order to rest and train. While he was there he made a play for a waitress working at the farm. In a fit of jealousy, the girl's boyfriend, Walter Dipley, shot him dead. The great middleweight was just 24.

AN ACTOR'S LIFE FOR ME!
2 – JOHNNY INDRISANO

Johnny Indrisano (1905–68) had a ten-year career as a welterweight, including a losing bout with world champion Jackie Fields, before becoming a boxing trainer to Hollywood film stars like Fred MacMurray. He appeared as a stuntman and small-part actor in dozens of movies and then secured a niche as a technical adviser on such fight films as *Body and Soul, The Set Up* and *The Kid From Brooklyn*. He tutored many young actors to look like fighters on screen. He is famed for his reply to one eager young thespian who asked how he was doing as a scrapper. 'Fine, just fine,' said Indrisano diplomatically. 'A word of advice, though – don't go starting no bar-room brawls!'

Ageism

In March 2008, Saoul Mamby, former super lightweight champion of the world between 1980 and 1982, lost on points to Anthony Osbourne over ten rounds in the Cayman Islands. Mamby was 60 years old, the oldest boxer to compete in a sanctioned match.

'I proved to the world that you don't have to be ashamed to be a senior citizen,' said George Foreman after going the 12 rounds' distance against champion Evander Holyfield at Atlantic City in 1991. Foreman was 45 when he became the oldest world heavyweight champion.

Frank Craig was a black American fighter who settled in Great Britain and mixed a boxing career with a music hall dancing act. He was born in 1868 and had his first professional contest in 1891. For a time he claimed the world coloured middleweight championship. More than 40 years later, when he was well over 60, he was still appearing in boxing booths around Great Britain.

The Comic Book Champions

The two best-known of comic-book boxing heroes were Joe Palooka in the USA and Rockfist Rogan in Great Britain.

Palooka was created by the cartoonist Hammond 'Ham' Fisher. He was based on a good-natured but inarticulate heavyweight Fisher had met in the 1920s. It took the boxer's creator a long time to sell his idea to an editor, but the first *Joe Palooka* comic strip originally appeared in 1930, when the well-meaning, gentle fighter won the world heavyweight championship with the aid of his manager, Knobby Walsh. Soon the adventures were being published in thousands of newspapers all over the world. In each story, against a boxing background, Joe Palooka defended people smaller than himself and stood up for their rights. He would only raise his fists against lawbreakers and bullies. He boxed in such colourful settings as the French Foreign Legion and, when America entered the war, he joined the US Army. The strip finally ceased publication in 1984.

Rockfist Rogan was a much tougher character than Palooka. He went actively looking for trouble. He was created by a veteran writer for comics called Frank S. Pepper, under the pen-name of Hal Wilton. The first story appeared in the *Champion* comic in 1938. At first the intrepid Rogan was a member of the Royal Flying Corps, but when war broke out the Spitfire pilot and amateur heavyweight transferred seamlessly to the RAF. Aided by a couple of devoted and loyal assistants he still continued to have adventures all over the world, as a typical title *Rockfist Rogan in the Kingdom of Khan* indicates. Even when he was made a prisoner of war, Rogan managed to outbox the German camp commandant, steal an aeroplane and escape. He never seemed to age or rise above the rank of Flight Lieutenant. The last edition of his adventures was published in the *Champion* in 1960, although his stories continued to be told in the *Tiger* for a little longer.

MICKEY ROURKE

A number of boxers have become film stars after careers as boxers, Oscar-winning Victor McLaglen among them. Mickey Rourke, however, was one of the few film actors to leave his screen work to enter the ring. After a spell as an amateur boxer, with 27 fights on his record, Rourke drifted into stage acting. He was recruited for his first film, *1941,* in 1979.

He achieved success as a tough-guy actor in such films as *Body Heat, Barfly* and *Angel Heart*. He developed a reputation as being a difficult actor on-set and his career went into a tailspin with such disasters as *Wild Orchid*.

In the early 1990s, already just over 40, Rourke decided to return to his ring career, this time as a professional. Fighting as a light heavyweight he cashed in on his film reputation to secure bouts in the USA, Germany and Japan. Over this period he won six and drew two lacklustre bouts. His already battered features were even further rearranged by his opponents, causing one writer to comment that it looked as if his head 'had been sculpted out of wet cat food.' In 2009, he made a surprise movie comeback with an excellent performance as an over-the-hill grappler in *The Wrestler,* for which he won a Golden Globe award and was nominated for a Best Actor award in the Oscars.

First Time Unlucky

Few boxers have been given a shot at the world heavyweight title in their first professional contests. Pete Rademacher was one of them. A former professional soldier and 1956 Melbourne Olympic gold medallist, he talked himself into a championship bout with champion Floyd Patterson. The title-holder was a fine boxer but notoriously had a glass jaw. At first the fight aroused some interest. Rademacher along with everyone else Patterson fought, was given a puncher's chance against the champion. He had lost only 7 of 79 amateur contests. Later, reality set in and the bout was largely regarded as a freak event.

Rademacher's amateur career was ended after he had won the Olympic final on a first-round stoppage. A US Army rule prevented Olympic winners from boxing competitively in the service. Rademacher did not want to become a coach, so he retired from the army.

An old army friend of the boxer's set up a syndicate of 22 business people, each contributing enough money for a total of $89,000 to promote Rademacher's courageous challenge to Patterson. They hired an experienced manager in Jack Hurley to advise them and to look after the technical details of the promotion.

Rademacher was to be paid $250,000 for his challenge on 22 August 1957. It was scheduled to take place at Sicks Stadium, a baseball park in Seattle. After the initial burst of publicity for the bizarre matchmaking, the promotion began to falter. The attendance was 16,691 and the gross receipts amounted to $143,000. Patterson had been guaranteed $250,000, while Jack Hurley's fee was $18,000. When it became apparent that the promotion was in danger, Patterson reduced his cut to $175,000 but this still left nothing for the challenger and his backers. Rademacher entered the ring a 50-1 underdog in the betting, aware that the promotion was scheduled to lose $120,000.

After a cautious opening round, true to form Rademacher knocked the vulnerable Patterson down in the second round. Patterson recovered to knock the challenger out in the sixth round. Rademacher became a journeyman heavyweight and then a successful businessman. Patterson won two more bouts and then lost his title to the Swedish heavyweight Ingemar Johansson, though he later recovered the title from him.

After the Patterson fight was over, one of Rademacher's handlers confirmed that the title challenge had largely been one of chutzpah. 'We was all lucky not to get thrown in jail,' he confessed.

CRACKS FROM COBB

Randall 'Tex' Cobb was a slightly above average journeyman heavyweight who plied his trade in the 1970s and '80s. He beat Earnie Shavers and lost to Larry Holmes and Buster Douglas. He became famous, however, for the wry one-liners with which he peppered his post-match interviews:

'All I do is hit somebody in the mouth. It's a whole lot easier than working for a living.'

'I've got my price – twenty-five cents and a loose woman.'

'You run for forty-five minutes, you train for an hour and a half. The rest of the time you hang out and talk tough.'

'I have more room for improvement than most heavyweights.'

'I had two years at college. I majored in probation.'

'Here's big, bad Earnie Shavers, probably the baddest man God ever allowed to walk on two legs, and he got up there with his bald head and his Fu Manchu and his bulging muscles and he stares at me. I cracked up. What did he think I was going to do, leave? Hell, if I was that scared I woulda left before then!'

'A return with Larry Holmes? I don't think his hands could stand the abuse!'

FIGHT FILMS – THE WORST:
1 – *KID NIGHTINGALE* (1939)

Director: George Amy **Screenplay:** Charles Belden
Leading Players: John Payne, Jane Wyman, Walter Catlett
A would-be opera singer forced to work as a waiter (Payne) takes up boxing. He starts singing from the ring after his bouts. He begins to hate the sport. In a big fight he is hit in the stomach. He cries out in pain, but the note emerging from his lungs is of such pure quality that an impresario in the crowd signs the boxer up as an opera singer. Crooner Payne makes an even less likely opera singer than he does a fighter.

COLLEGE BOYS: 2 – VERNON SCANNELL

Vernon Scannell (1922–2007) was a poet and novelist who sometimes wrote about boxing. He left school at the age of 14, but not before he had reached the final of the British Schoolboy Championships.

He served with the Gordon Highlanders in the Second World War, saw action in North Africa, took part in the Normandy landings, was wounded, twice deserted and served time in a military prison. While he was on the run he earned his living as a professional middleweight boxer. His poems attracted the attention of two professors at Leeds University, who secured a place for him there. Ignoring the fact that he had been a professional, Scannell boxed for his university and won the Northern Universities' welterweight, middleweight and light heavyweight championships.

THE GREAT CHAMPIONS:
3 – HENRY ARMSTRONG: 1912–88

Main weights: featherweight, lightweight, welterweight
Contests: 180 **Won:** 149 (KO:101) **Lost:** 21 **Drew:** 10
Henry Armstrong, aka 'Homicide Hank' and 'the Human Buzz-Saw' held world titles at three different weights – featherweight, lightweight and welterweight – over a short period of time and came close to taking a fourth. The possessor of an abnormally slow heart-rate, he was able to fight fifteen rounds at an incredibly fast rate, seldom stopping punching. He had a number of contests as an amateur and then hitchhiked from St Louis to Los Angeles to turn professional under the name of Melody Jackson. As a black fighter he had to box to order, losing when he was told to do so. His all-action style attracted the attention of singer and fight-fan Al Jolson, who recommended the fighter to manager Eddie Mead. Mead changed the youngster's name to Henry Armstrong, to distance him from his lacklustre Melody Jackson image. 1937 turned out to be a magical year for the unleashed 'Armstrong'. He won 27 contests, 26 of them inside the distance, and started homing in on a clutch of titles. In turn he won the featherweight, welterweight and lightweight championships and fought a draw for the middleweight title. Unable to make the weight, Armstrong gave up the featherweight title and lost the lightweight crown to Lou Ambers. He then concentrated on fighting as a welterweight. He defended it 19 times, 15 inside the distance.

No man could fight at Armstrong's pace for ever. Finally he began to slow down. He lost his remaining title to Fritzie Zivic, retired for a while and then came back to take part in

49 contests over the next three years. After his retirement he toured the Far East with a forces' entertainment unit for a time. He lost most of his money but then became the minister of a church. He died blind and in poverty.

THE MISSING BELT

John L. Sullivan was the last of the American bare-knuckle champions. He was so popular that in 1887 the citizens of Boston, his home city, clubbed together to present him with a magnificent gold-plated championship belt studded with hundreds of diamonds. It was estimated to be worth $10,000. A profligate, fast-living man, Sullivan often pawned his belt but always retrieved it or got friends to do it for him.

After his death it went missing for a time. It was rumoured that it was in the possession of another heavyweight, Jim Barry, a former protégé of Sullivan's. Barry, a brave, reckless fighter, was even wilder than his mentor. He would fight anyone but was a drug addict and a heavy drinker. In 1917, he was knocked out in Panama City by Sam McVea. The following day Jim Barry was shot and killed in a bar-room brawl in Colón, Panama.

Some years later, John L. Sullivan's belt was found and purchased by the Smithsonian Institute. None of the hundreds of diamonds remained. Did Jim Barry sell them in Panama, or perhaps hide the diamonds, intending to collect them one day?

PURSES

In 1944, in New York, leading lightweights Beau Jack and Bob Montgomery fought. Tickets were only available to those who bought war bonds. 15,822 bonds were sold. Jack and Montgomery were both privates in the US Army. Neither man would take any money for the bout, but each was given a token purse of one dollar. Jack won the ten-round bout on points.

FOUL! 2 – JOE BYGRAVES

A Welsh referee called Mr English had an exciting night in 1953. The occasion was an international amateur match between England and Wales. Mr English had only two matches at which to officiate. They each involved a leading English heavyweight, Henry Cooper and Joe Bygraves. English caused something of a sensation by disqualifying both the English prospects.

He caused even more of a sensation when he returned ill-advisedly to the dressing room. The waiting and extremely incensed Bygraves knocked the official out with a mighty right-hand. The boxer was banned from amateur fighting for life. He turned professional. As the phlegmatic Cooper pointed out, he didn't have anywhere else to go.

BREAKING IN

Bare-knuckle champion Daniel Mendoza got his start in prize fighting when he was working in a teashop. The proprietor of the shop was attacked by a patron, who was ejected by Mendoza. Richard Humphries, a professional fighter, was passing by. He was so impressed by Mendoza's fighting abilities that he recommended that the 16-year-old youth should become a professional fighter. Later the two men had four epic contests, each winning two.

Freddy Foreman, a British career criminal, was encouraged to enter the ring when, as a young man, he shared a cell with two professional boxers. He was so inspired by the tales of their fighting lives that he decided to become a professional as soon as he was released. For his first paid contest he was matched in 1954 at the Manor Place Baths in London against Del Breen, an experienced welterweight. Foreman took such a beating that he never fought again.

LAST ORDERS

After his retirement from the ring, heavyweight Brian London opened the 007 night club in Blackpool. It achieved fame in January 1971 when the mighty West Ham football team arrived at Blackpool to play a cup match against the home side, which was bottom of its division. On the night before the match, four West Ham players, Bobby Moore, Jimmy Greaves, Brian Dear and Clyde Best spent part of the night drinking at the club. The players were fined by West Ham. Blackpool won the cup-tie 4–0.

ENTRANCE MUSIC

Muhammad Ali was the first well-known boxer to enter the ring to the tune of a popular song. In 1977, when he fought

Earnie Shavers, the public address system played the theme of *Star Wars*. Other fighters soon copied this example:

'Ain't No Stopping Us Now'	Larry Holmes
'Overjoyed'	Floyd Mayweather Jr.
'My Way'	Bernard Hopkins
'Unbeaten'	Joe Calzaghe
'Two Tribes Go to War'	Travis Lutter
'Get Up, Stand Up!'	Razor Ruddock
'The Stars and Stripes for Ever'	Marvin Hagler
'Hail to the Victors'	Thomas Hearns
'It Takes Two'	Michael Moorer

As early as 1947, Scottish flyweight Vic Herman provided a do-it-yourself entrance accompaniment. He entered the ring playing the bagpipes.

ENDING IN TEARS

In Las Vegas in 1997, heavyweight Oliver McCall was stopped in five rounds by Lennox Lewis. The official reason for the stoppage was that McCall had 'refused to defend himself'. The bout was for the World Boxing Council's vacant world heavyweight title. McCall seemed to suffer some form of nervous breakdown in the ring. He boxed well enough for the first two rounds; in the third round, however, the American heavyweight burst into tears. For almost a minute he stood without defending himself as Lewis pummelled him. At the end of the round McCall refused to return to his corner. He walked around the ring grimacing and weeping. In the fourth round practically nothing happened. A perplexed Lewis was reluctant to hit an opponent who plainly did not want to fight. Referee Mills Lane shouted to McCall, 'Do you want to fight?' At the end of the round, Lane led the American back to his corner, where McCall sobbed to his seconds, 'I don't want to go out there again!' His seconds persuaded him to try one more round, but again McCall refused to throw a punch. After 55 seconds the referee stopped the contest, declaring a bewildered Lewis to be the winner.

FIGHT FILMS – THE BEST:
2 – *THE SET UP* (1949)

Director: Robert Wise **Screenplay:** Art Cohn **Leading Players:** Robert Ryan (Stoker Thompson), Audrey Totter (Julie), George Tobias (Tiny) and Alan Baxter (Little Boy)

The action of the film takes place in and around a sleazy boxing stadium on the night of a tournament. It is set in 'real time' over the couple of hours that the bill lasts. Over-the-hill heavyweight Stoker (Robert Ryan) has been bribed to take a dive, but his venal handlers, wanting to hold on to all the cash, have not bothered to tell their man, convinced that he will lose anyhow. Instead Stoker puts up the fight of his life, wins the contest and has his hands smashed by the vengeful mobsters.

The film provides a magnificent depiction of the ambience of the losers among the boxers, hangers-on and spectators, with nothing to live for except their regular adrenalin fix at the stadium. Ryan, a former college champion, is magnificent as a proud but inarticulate man who maintains his standards no matter what.

Fighting Talk

Over the years a number of words and phrases originating in boxing have entered the English language for more general use. Some of them have been altered in the transition. For example, in 1900 former heavyweight champion Bob Fitzsimmons was scheduled to fight gigantic Ed Dunkhorst, 'the Human Freight Car', who weighed 250lb. This meant that Fitzsimmons was scheduled to give away more than 50lb in weight and 4 inches in height. When asked if he was worried about these discrepancies the 37-year-old, one-time champion at middleweight and heavyweight, shrugged and said, 'The bigger they are, the heavier they fall!' This was later transmogrified to 'the *harder* they fall!' It became a common response from anyone forced to take on a superior opponent. While phrases can have a number of different origins, other common sayings which may relate to boxing are:

Throwing in the towel: to surrender. This was derived from a practice common in the 1880s, when a second could withdraw a battered fighter from a contest by tossing a towel into the ring.

Throwing your hat into the ring: to challenge someone. Its origin dates back to bare-knuckle days, when a fighter making his way to the ring would throw his hat over the ropes ahead of him as a sign of defiance.

Below the belt: to take unfair advantage. To hit an opponent below the belt, or to deliver a low blow, was a foul in all sorts of boxing.

Leading with your chin: to invite trouble. A boxer who did not guard his chin was regarded as most unwary.

Saved by the bell: to be rescued in the nick of time. Under the Queensberry Rules, the count ended over a boxer who had been knocked down when the bell went to signify the end of a round. This was amended in 1963 when several bodies allowed the referee to continue counting after the bell.

Haymaker: a wild-swinging punch. At the beginning of the twentieth century a journalist used this to describe a blow delivered in a boxing match in an arc, like the swinging of a scythe when cutting hay. 'Haymaker' then entered the language as a description of a hard punch.

Whip-round: to collect money for a good cause. Whips were stewards who controlled unruly bare-knuckle crowds with the use of whips if need be. Sometimes the whips would pass round a hat for coins to be thrown in for a particularly brave fighter.

Rope-a-dope: to confuse someone by being unorthodox. In Kinshasa, Zaire, in 1974, Muhammad Ali regained his title by the apparently bizarre method of spending much of the time leaning back on the ropes allowing his opponent George Foreman to punch himself out in the humid atmosphere. When Foreman was exhausted, Ali knocked him out.

AN ACTOR'S LIFE FOR ME! 3 – FREDDIE STEELE

Freddie Steele had lost only two bouts out of over a hundred when he won the world middleweight championship by outpointing Babe Risko over 15 rounds in 1936. His fighting career came to an end when he suffered a horrendous injury against Fred Apostoli two years later. Steele broke his breastbone and soon had to retire from boxing.

He broke into movies by acting as a boxing double in the fight scenes for Errol Flynn as early heavyweight champion James J. Corbett in *Gentleman Jim* (1942). Flynn was so unfit that he could only box for about a minute at a time. Steele's tough-looking, mangled face led to his being cast as tough soldiers or hoodlums in such films as *The Story of G.I. Joe, Hail the Conquering Hero* and *Call Northside 777*.

PUNCHING POWER

A hard punch does not necessarily mean that a boxer will become a champion. In the 1960s, LaMar Clark, a chicken farmer from Cedar City, Utah, went on a spree of wins with 44 consecutive knockouts, gaining him a national reputation. However, he was very carefully matched in these contests by his backers, mainly against a series of local hard cases, novices and wrestlers. When he stepped up a notch in class, Clark was beaten several times. The end came to his career came when he was matched against the young Cassius Clay (later Muhammad Ali). Clay knocked him out and Clark retired from boxing at the age of 27.

CELEBRITY BOXING

Boxing has always been closely allied to show business. In 2002, efforts were made in the USA and Great Britain to run a series of three-round contests between well-known people, with the winners donating their purses to charity. In the event, most of the so-called celebrities turned out to be of the minor variety and definitely from yesteryear.

In the USA, former players from such long-forgotten television series as *The Brady Bunch*, *The Partridge Family* and *Diff'rent Strokes* sparred tentatively, wearing helmets and 16-ounce gloves. The main event was between skater Tonya Harding, who had been found guilty of planning an attack meant to disable one of her Olympic rivals, and Paula Jones, who had launched a sexual harassment claim against former US President Bill Clinton. The fight was extremely one-sided, with a tearful Jones asking for it to be stopped in the third round.

The format was taken up in Great Britain by the BBC. The main event was between entrepreneur Grant Bovey and comedian Ricky Gervais, two less than sylph-like competitors. The bout was won by Gervais, who, with some accuracy, summarised the fight as being like watching two sea-lions making love.

BROTHERLY LOVE

Mike and Tom Gibbons were two superb boxers from St Paul, Minnesota, in the opening decades of the twentieth century. Tom, a heavyweight, lost only four of over 100 contests and went the full 15-round distance with Jack Dempsey for the world heavyweight title.

Mike, a lighter man, was even better. He was generally regarded as the most brilliant boxer of his era. He was aware of this fact and not slow to remind his brother of his superiority.

Once they were hired to fight each other in an exhibition contest. Mike choreographed their movements beforehand.

'In the third round you knock me down for a short count,' he explained. 'Great,' beamed Tom, 'and when do you knock me down?'

'Whenever I damn well want to,' said Mike shortly.

DAMAGES

Heavyweight Lou Nova had been a colourful heavyweight contender in the 1930s and '40s. He had gained a great deal of publicity by claiming to have been a devotee of yoga and to have developed a stunning 'cosmic punch' from his mentor, Oom the Omnipotent. Nova had secured a title fight with Joe Louis in 1941 but had been stopped in six rounds.

Fourteen years later, in 1955, a *Los Angeles Examiner* writer wrote an article about the fight. He described the boxer's behaviour in the contest as being that of a frightened, screaming child. Nova, who had become an actor, was appearing in a Manhattan production of the hit musical *Guys and Dolls,* as a gangster. He sued the writer and the Hearst Publishing Company for libel, claiming $200,000.

During the hearing, lawyers for the writer produced other sports writers who confirmed Nova's rather nervous showing against the world champion more than a decade before. During cross-examination Nova was forced to admit that both his cosmic punch and Oom the Omnipotent had been figments of his press agent's imagination. He provided examples of his courage in the ring against such leading heavyweights as Max Baer and Tony Galento.

After deliberating for three hours, the jury decided that it had been unfair to dub Nova a coward. They awarded him a settlement of $35,000.

Fight Films – The Worst:
2 – *Tennessee Champ* (1954)

Director: Fred M. Wilcox **Screenplay:** Art Cohn **Leading Players:** Dewey Martin, Shelley Winters, Keenan Wynn, Charles Buchinksy (Charles Bronson)

A minister's son (Martin) goes on the run after he thinks he has killed a man in a brawl. He is taken up by a crooked boxing manager and becomes a fighter. He is matched for the biggest fight of his career and discovers that his opponent is the man he thinks he has killed. After a fierce contest, the minister's son wins, gives up the ring and takes over his father's church as the new minister.

A number of lapses in credibility are apparent, including the fact that the rippling-muscled Bronson, defeated in the climactic bout, looks as if he could eat the minister's son alive.

Foul! 3 – Fritzie Zivic

Even the toughest of professional fighters drew the line somewhere. Fritzie Zivic was regarded as the wildest fighter of his time, but even he had his limits: 'I'd give 'em the head and choke 'em, but I never used the thumb, because I didn't want them to use the thumb on me,' he once declared self-righteously.

The Great Champions:
4 – Muhammad Ali: 1941–Present

Main weight: heavyweight **Contests:** 61 **Won:** 56 (KO:37) **Lost:** 5 **Drew:** 0

Muhammad Ali, born Cassius Clay and known as 'the Greatest', dominated boxing in the 1960s and '70s with his charm, charisma, speed, courage and boxing ability. He attracted to the sport millions who would never otherwise have had any interest in boxing. After an outstanding amateur career, in which he won several national Golden Gloves titles and took a gold medal in the light heavyweight division at the 1960s Rome Olympics, he turned professional. His trainer, the experienced Angelo Dundee, recognised the natural ability of his protégé and preserved his original fluid style, concentrating on getting him to 'sit down' on his punching in order to give it more power.

Clay, as he was at first known, rattled off a series of victories. He became a great favourite of the media and the public when he started making up doggerel predicting the round in which his next opponent would be knocked out.

In 1964 he pulled off an enormous upset by defeating the frightening Sonny Liston in eight rounds to take the heavyweight championship. Fifteen months later he defeated Liston again, this time in a single round.

The champion became a Muslim and changed his name to Muhammad Ali. He defended his title successfully with ease on a number of occasions against all the leading challengers. In 1967, he was stripped of his title by the WBA and the New York Athletic Commission for refusing to be conscripted into the US Army, saying that he had no quarrel with the Viet Cong. He was not allowed to fight again in the USA for three years. In 1970, he made a comeback but, ring-rusty, he lost to Joe Frazier in 1971. Gradually he fought his way back to the top, defeating Joe Frazier in a return and then regaining his title by defeating George Foreman in the 'Rumble in the Jungle' in Zaire.

Surprisingly, he lost his title again in 1978 but took it back, becoming world heavyweight champion for the third time. He defeated Frazier in the 'Thriller in Manila', rated one of the greatest of all heavyweight bouts. He retired once more. He returned two years later at the age of 38 but was only a shadow of his former self and lost to Larry Holmes in 11 one-sided rounds. He retired again and in later life he suffered from Parkinson's Disease.

Where Did it All Go?

'Iron' Mike Tyson was heavyweight champion from 1986, when he was only 20 years old, until 1990 and then again briefly in 1996. He was the most feared boxer of his era, with a knockout punch in either hand and capable of steamrollering over any opponent.

However, his private life was turbulent, full of street brawls, messy and expensive divorce settlements and prison sentences for rape and road rage. He was reputed to have earned more money than any other boxer, ever – something in the region of £200 million. Yet by 2003, when he was 37 years old and still fighting for a living, he claimed to be $5 million in debt and to have only a few thousand dollars in his bank account. He filed for bankruptcy, claiming that his lifestyle was costing him £200,000 a month.

Accountants scrutinising the few documents Tyson had kept, estimated that among his spending sprees the following items were included:

Managers, agents	£60 million
Gifts to friends	£10 million
IRS Tax owed	£8 million
State taxes owed	£1 million

Houses	£8 million
Divorce settlement (i)	£7 million
Divorce settlement (ii)	6 million
Cars	£4 million
Legal fees and fines	£3 million
Wristwatch	£1 million
Parties	£1 million
Gambling	£1 million

Tyson also owed child maintenance and unpaid salaries. His wagebill was immense; in one year he paid an aide called 'Crocodile' £150,000 to attend pre-fight press conferences and shout 'Guerrilla Warfare' at intervals. 'I'm not tight with a dollar' sighed the ex-champion when he retired from boxing in 2005. 'Everybody's got a game plan until he gets hit in the mouth.'

SPARRING PARTNERS

The job of sparring partner was once rated in a poll as the third most dangerous in the world, after high-wire walking and lion taming. It has never paid well and usually attracts fighters on the slide when they cannot get regular contests. Now and again, however, a sparring partner has disconcerted the professional who is supposed to beat him up on a daily basis. After Mark Kaylor had lost to the younger James Cook he said sadly, 'During my prime, James had been one of my sparring partners, paid to get the crap beaten out of him.'

Between 1909 and 1920, Sid Burns was a highly-rated welterweight who fought for the British and Commonwealth titles and had gone in with such outstanding boxers as Georges Carpentier. While he was at the peak of his career he recruited a young beginner called Ted 'Kid' Lewis as a sparring partner. He punished the tyro severely during their training sessions but Lewis admitted that he had learned a great deal from the older fighter. Years later, their positions were reversed. Lewis had become a world champion and he hired the veteran Burns as a sparring partner.

One of the great mysteries in the world of sparring partners is what really happened when world heavyweight champion Joe Louis employed Jersey Joe Walcott while he was training for his return match with the German Max Schmeling in 1938. Walcott, already an experienced boxer but with no connections, left the training camp hastily after a few days. Louis's handlers said that it was because Walcott was not good enough to face the heavy-punching champion. Walcott, on the other hand, let it be known that he was dismissed because he had shown Louis up and dropped him with a left hook. A decade later, both men met in earnest twice for the world crown. In their first bout, Louis won a highly controversial points decision. In the return match Louis retained his title on a knockout in the 11th round. After Louis's retirement, Jersey Joe eventually became the world heavyweight champion.

Featherweight Willie Pep is rated as one of the most skilful boxers of all time. He turned professional in 1940. Early in his career, desperate for money and with a wife and family to support, he took a job as a dollar-a-round sparring partner to future world bantamweight champion Manuel Ortiz. Several years later, in 1944, Pep and Ortiz were matched in a genuine contest. Ortiz's manager disdained Pep's challenge. 'We paid the guy three dollars a day and he wasn't worth much more,' he declared. Pep defeated Ortiz on a unanimous decision. This time he received $20,000 for going into the ring with the Mexican.

Sparring partners never had it easy. When Vernon Ball was hired to spar with the Welsh flyweight champion Norman Lewis, he found that Lewis always used a pair of gloves from which the padding had worked away from the knuckles. This considerably improved the effectiveness of the champion's punching power and he wreaked havoc on the hired hands.

For many years heavyweight champion Muhammad Ali employed husky Larry Holmes as his sparring partner. The two men got on well together. In 1979, Ali retired. Holmes became the champion. In 1980 Ali made a comeback and challenged a reluctant Holmes for the title. By this time, Ali was over the hill. He took a dreadful beating while a distracted Holmes let him go the distance. Afterwards, a remorseful Holmes visited the battered Ali in the latter's dressing room. 'I love you, Muhammad,' he mumbled. The irrepressible Ali looked quizzically at the victor. 'If you love me, why did you beat up on me?' he demanded through swollen lips.

Fred 'Nosher' Powell was hired to act as sparring partner to the gigantic Cuban heavyweight Nino Valdez. He suspected that on the final day of sparring, Valdez was really going to unload on him. As soon as the final session started, Powell bounded across the ring and hit the Cuban in the face with all the power he could muster. At the same time he uttered a howl of agony and shook his fist, claiming to have broken his hand. Valdez's manager begged Powell to continue, but the prudent sparring partner refused to entertain the foolhardy notion.

The Irish amateur middleweight Terry Christle qualified as a doctor in Dublin and turned professional, billed as 'the Fighting Physician'. In 1987, he worked as a sparring partner to Marvin Hagler. One day Hagler complained of feeling unwell and asked Christle for a professional opinion. Christle recommended bed-rest for Hagler and a day off for himself.

Idi Amin

Boxing has attracted followers from all walks of life. Idi Amin, who began a brutal reign as dictator in Uganda after leading a military coup in 1971, was a close follower of the sport and even won the Ugandan Open Heavyweight title on three occasions. He was not, however, quite as successful as he and a number of biographers stated. He boasted that he had never been defeated by a European in the ring. He was in fact defeated twice by colonial police officer Les Peach.

Up and Down

Between 1930 and 1931, a French-Canadian former lumberjack called Elzear Roux had nine heavyweight contests in Britain, winning eight of them. He defeated a number of good second-class fighters, including Marine Bill Trinder (twice), Jack Humbeeck and Ted Mason, and looked impressive in the process. When it became known that earlier in his career Roux had encountered such top-class men as Tom Heeney and Jim Maloney, fight followers began to wonder why such a good-quality performer had left the USA to practise his trade in Europe.

Then the news filtered out. Shortly before making a hurried departure from North America, Roux had gone into the ring with the gigantic Primo Carnera, who was being groomed by the mob for a world title shot. The enormous

Italian was being fed on a diet of 'divers' who were being paid or menaced to make him look good. Roux had been one of the first opponents to come to an 'arrangement' with Carnera's backers. He had met Carnera in Chicago in January 1930. 18,000 people had paid almost $60,000 to see the so-called fight. The bout had lasted 47 seconds. In that time Roux had visited the canvas on six separate occasions. What was odd about the contest was not the fact that Roux had not landed a single punch in that time, but ringside spectators had sworn that they had not seen the cumbersome Carnera deliver one blow either.

The Illinois Boxing Commission had fined the Canadian $1,000 for his inept performance and had revoked his licence for twelve months. Unable to secure bouts in the USA, Roux had decided to try his luck in Great Britain, far from the ministrations of the really dangerous gangsters.

ALPHABET SOUP

Over the years a number of competing controlling bodies have sprung up to control the game – and extract sanctioning fees from fighters and promoters. Each organisation appoints its own champions, rates fighters and issues belts. This means that whereas once there were only eight officially recognised title-holders, today there are dozens. The major organisations are:

World Boxing Association
Originally known as the National Boxing Association, it changed its name in 1962 because so many overseas bodies were affiliating to it. In 1981, a boxing judge claimed that he been paid by officers of the association to favour certain

fighters. Eyebrows were also raised when Argentinian welterweight Juan Martin Coggi was rated more highly than his record would seem to merit. Coggi went on to win the title. In 1996, against Frankie Randall, Coggi refused to fight on after a clash of heads. He was awarded the victory on a 'technical decision'.

World Boxing Council

Set up in 1963 to rival the WBA because non-USA members felt that overseas members were being ignored, it now has a majority of delegates from Latin America. In 1992, heavyweight Riddick Bowe notoriously embarrassed the organisation by dumping his WBC belt in a trash can at a press conference rather than fight Lennox Lewis. Journalists and others have not been above trying to embarrass the sanctioning bodies in order to get a laugh or a story. Two journalists once almost got a prince in Saudi Arabia, who had never boxed, ranked by the World Boxing Council. The two writers knew that the prince was being taught to box by a professional. Mischievously, they told the president of the council that the prince was a new star in Middle Eastern boxing circles. The credulous official offered to put the member of the royal family into the world rankings as number eight. The prince's trainer firmly placed a veto on the suggestion. If the royal family heard that the prince was a ranked fighter they might insist on his boxing someone, in which case he would be badly damaged. Reluctantly the writers abandoned their plan, announcing that the prince had retired from active competition.

World Boxing Organisation

Set up in 1988 by a Puerto Rican breakaway group from the WBA. It survived criticism in 1989 for refusing to recognise

Mike Tyson as heavyweight champion, preferring its own nominee. It reached the headlines again in 2001 when it moved a boxer called Darrin Morris up in the ratings, despite the fact that he was dead.

International Boxing Federation
Formed in 1983, its rules stipulated that its president must be an American. It came under a cloud in 1999 when one of its officers was accused of accepting bribes to move boxers up in the ratings.

FIGHT FILMS – THE BEST: 3 – *FAT CITY* (1972)

Director: John Huston **Screenplay:** Leonard Gardner **Leading Players:** Stacy Keach, Jeff Bridges, Susan Tyrrell, Nicholas Colasanto, Art Aragon
The lives of two boxers, an embittered alcoholic veteran played by Stacy Keach and a naïve young hopeful portrayed by Jeff Bridges, intertwine against a background of the small-time Stockton, California, fight clubs. The film is short on plot but long on atmosphere and character. Huston, a fight fan and former amateur lightweight, employed a number of real pugs at $150 a day as set dressing. Keach, in a role originally intended for Marlon Brando, is outstanding. The final fight sequence between Keach and Sixto Rodriquez, a Puerto Rican light heavyweight of the 1960s, is one of the most realistic ever put on the screen. In a non-speaking part, Rodriguez is impressive. He is seen urinating blood before his bout even begins, but presents a picture of a battered man who has seen everything but has managed to retain his dignity.

'Fits You Nicely, Sir!'

Light heavyweight John Conteh was delighted when he was told that he was going to box in one of the supporting contests to the Muhammad Ali–Alvin Lewis heavyweight bout at a Dublin stadium in 1972. In the event he was not quite so pleased. First, in the dressing room before his fight, an official attempted to force both of Conteh's hands into left-handed boxing gloves. In vain Conteh tried to tell the Irishman that he was struggling with two left-handed gloves. The obdurate official refused to listen to the increasingly irate boxer. In the end Conteh had to threaten to hit the official before the man went off reluctantly to fetch the correct gloves. The whole business took much more time than had been allocated. Then the route to the ring across the stadium was such a long one that the boxer and his entourage practically had to run across the field. Even so, they were still late arriving, to the annoyance of the crowd. When the bout finally started, the first round seemed to go on forever to Conteh. Finally it was discovered that both clocks prepared for the timekeeper had stopped. The bout then had to be halted for another long period while the clocks were repaired. The only good thing about the evening as far as the Liverpool boxer was concerned was that he won his bout in the long-delayed second round.

College Boys: 3 – The Klitschko Brothers

Vitali and Wladimir Klitschko, from the Ukraine, were two of the most popular and successful heavyweights of their time. Both were huge. Vitali was 6ft 7in tall while his brother was 2in shorter. They had outstanding amateur records and both went on to win versions of the world professional heavyweight title.

They were the well-educated sons of an air force colonel and both of them received doctorates in sports studies from Kiev University. Opportunistic promoter Don King offered them $100 million if they would fight each other in the ring. The brothers refused.

MEN OF THE CLOTH: 1 – BENDIGO

A number of champions have taken to religion after retirement from the ring. Several have even become ministers.

William Thompson (1811–80), better known as Bendigo, was a brave bare-knuckle champion and a completely irresponsible man. Brought up in a workhouse, he took to fighting with enthusiasm and soon gained a reputation as one of the dirtiest of ring practitioners. He anticipated Muhammad Ali by more than a century, 'trash talking' and reviling opponents in order to get them into the ring with him. Kicking, gouging and elbowing were all parts of his ring technique.

Outside of the ring he was a prominent member of a gang of street ruffians, known as the Nottingham Lambs. He is said to have been imprisoned on almost 30 occasions for different criminal offences.

However, when Bendigo retired from the ring he became a travelling evangelist. He claimed to have been converted to Christianity by a sermon delivered by one of the many prison chaplains with whom he came into contact. Upon his release he joined a sect known as the Good Templars. He came under the influence of a fiery preacher called

'Undaunted Dick' Weaver. Bendigo admitted that he had 'fought and sinned for the Devil for 62 years,' and that now he was going to serve Jesus Christ. He travelled the countryside preaching, or backing up more accomplished speakers, drawing the crowds by displaying his prize belts and cups won in the ring and later retrieved from various pawnbrokers. There were reports that he was not above descending from the pulpit and hitting rowdies trying to break up his meetings.

In London's Whitechapel he once drew a crowd estimated as being in the region of 2,000 people. In his later years he became a familiar sight in Nottingham market place, drawing large crowds and handing out religious tracts.

Time to Go

Some boxers have stayed on in the game for too long. Others have been able to take the hint when it was time to go.

Former world light heavyweight champion José Torres (1936–2009) was coming to the end of his career when he was matched with journeyman Jimmy Ralston at Madison Square Garden in 1969. Ralston withdrew without any notice. The promoter, Teddy Brenner, rushed out into the street and encountered Charley 'Devil' Green passing by. Green was a former sparring partner of Torres'. Brenner offered him $3,500 to come in and fight the former champion. Green agreed with alacrity. He faced up to Torres and knocked the light heavyweight down twice in the first two rounds. Torres came back to knock Green out in the second round, but he knew that the writing was on the wall. He retired from boxing to follow a successful career as a fight commentator, author and Head of the New York State Athletic Commission.

COMMENTATORS

Reg Gutteridge (1924–2009) was for many years the boxing commentator for ITV's *World of Sport*. He even secured a brief and breathless interview with world champion Muhammad Ali in the interval between rounds of one of his fights.

In 1967, he was covering the world amateur championships in Rome for ITV. Having an afternoon off, Gutteridge noticed that the England team was being taken to a wine-tasting. However, the commentator boarded the Irish team's coach by mistake and was taken to the Vatican for an audience with the Pope.

Gutteridge once interviewed the sullen and uncommunicative heavyweight champion Sonny Liston. Exasperated by the boxer's taciturn responses Gutteridge stood up, picked up a fork from the table and stabbed it viciously into his leg, exclaiming, 'So you think you're hard!' He then stalked out of the room, with the fork still jammed in his leg. Later it was explained to the still stunned Liston that the commentator had lost a limb when he had stepped on a land mine at the Normandy landings and that his right leg was made of wood.

QUIET, PLEASE!

In 1922, middleweight Harry Greb was scheduled to meet heavyweight Tommy Gibbons at Madison Square Garden in New York. Supporters of both fighters clashed in the lobby of the Pennsylvania Hotel in New York. Security staff and the police were unable to separate the two gangs. What they did not know was that Greb was trying to rest in one of the hotel rooms before the fight. He suddenly appeared in the lobby, menacingly asking for quiet. He got it. Both sets of fans tiptoed quietly out into the street.

MOUNTAIN MEN

Some of the toughest of all bare-knuckle fighters were the notorious mountain men who fought on the sides of hills and mountains in Wales towards the end of the nineteenth century and beginning of the twentieth century. Many of them were miners earning a few extra shillings, although a few were full-time fighters. Some of their contests were shocking in their brutality, even for their times. One form of mountain fighting consisted of two contestants being buried up to their waists in the earth, facing one another, so that they could not move their feet. They then fought it out, directing fearsome blows to the head, until one of the combatants was unconscious.

Some of the mountain fighters attained more than local fame. Ianto Pom Pom, Shoni Engineer and Gomer Evans were leading participants. One of the most feared was Lewis Roderick, who went mad from taking too many blows to the head. When a group of policemen tried to arrest him they found that his misshapen wrists were too thick for their handcuffs.

Redmond Coleman of Georgetown, 'the Iron Man from Iron Lane', was arrested a total of 127 times for drunkenness.

Deaths in the mountain contests were not uncommon and a number of victors served time in prison for manslaughter.

FUSS AND BOTHER

In 1990, undisputed World Heavyweight Champion Mike Tyson made a routine defence of his title against journeyman James 'Buster' Douglas in Tokyo. Douglas was so poorly regarded that bookmakers laid odds of 42-1 against his winning.

At first matters went according to plan. Tyson caught up with his opponent in the eighth round and knocked Douglas down for a long count. However, the champion was beset by personal and legal problems and lost concentration. Slowly Douglas started getting on top. In the tenth round he released a flurry of punches and knocked Tyson down for the first time in his career. Tyson failed to beat the count and referee declared Douglas the winner.

If the fight had been unusual, what happened next was even more bizarre. Promoter Don King and his acolytes, seeing the treasured heavyweight championship slipping away from their grasp, did everything in their power to get the decision reversed. King had shown partisanship from the start. After Douglas had got up from his long count in the eight round the promoter screamed at one of the WBC officials, 'What kind of referee did you bring with you from Mexico? You're going to get my man beat!'

After the bout, King held several press conferences in which he accused the referee, Octavio Meyran, of allowing Douglas to remain on the canvas for more than the permitted ten seconds. King insisted that the fight be declared null and void and that the two heavyweights should meet in the ring again. He pressurised the WBC and WBA to withhold their recognition of Douglas's claim to the title, which they did for several days.

Douglas was distraught but calmer heads prevailed. The bout had been covered by most of the world's leading sports writers. They were of the opinion that James 'Buster' Douglas had won fairly and was entitled to the championship. They said so firmly in their columns. Don King and the sanctioning officials backed down and admitted that Douglas was the official undisputed world heavyweight champion.

It was a brief moment of glory for the new champion. Douglas allowed the adulation following his win to go to his head. He neglected his training and ballooned up to a great weight. He defended his championship for the first time against Evander Holyfield and lost it in three rounds.

'MORE GORE!'

The patrons of the aristocratic National Sporting Club in London at the beginning of the twentieth century were a well-behaved set. They were not allowed to cheer while a round was in progress and had to abide by other rules of decorum. However, they were determined to get value for money. If they thought that a contest was too dull, despite the frowns of the club's administrators, they would call disapprovingly in well-modulated accents, 'More gore!'

JACK DEMPSEY V. COWBOY LUTTRALL

By 1940, the former great heavyweight champion Jack Dempsey was running a restaurant in New York, but still needed to go on the road from time to time refereeing wrestling matches in order to make a few extra dollars. One night he was officiating at a tag-team match in Atlanta when he pushed mat villain Clarence 'Cowboy' Luttrall in order to make the grappler stand off his opponent. Luttrall took exception to this and swung a punch at the former champion. Dempsey ducked the blow easily and thought no more of the matter. Afterwards, in the dressing room, he tried to placate the veteran Luttrall. The wrestler stalked away. A few days later he issued a public challenge to Dempsey, the latter to wear boxing gloves while Luttrall wrestled. Max Waxman, Dempsey's agent at the time, saw a chance to gain some publicity and a few extra dollars for his client and accepted the challenge on the fighter's behalf. Dempsey, who seemed bewildered by the whole affair, confirmed that the bout would be for real. 'It's no gag,' he assured reporters. Luttrall, seeing his chance for his fifteen minutes of fame, was more forthcoming. 'I'm going to knock his front teeth out,' he threatened. The bout, attracting 12,000 spectators, was an anti-climax. Dempsey lumbered after the inept Luttrall from the opening bell, smashed his opponent to the canvas four times and in the second round knocked the wrestler completely out of the ring. Luttrall cracked his head on a camera case and could not get back into the ring in time. He received $800 for his evening's work but he did not achieve the notoriety for which he had been hoping. The bout had been refereed by Nat Fleischer, the editor of *Ring* magazine. In his newspaper reports on the bout, Fleischer mis-spelt the Cowboy's name as Luttrell.

THREATS

'I'll moida da bum!'
Tony Galento before losing in four rounds to heavyweight champion Joe Louis, 1939.

'I've got nothing against him, he's a nice guy, but I want to kill him!'
Rocky Graziano before losing his third world title fight against Tony Zale in 1948.

'From now on he fights his wife!'
Disgusted manager Alex Koskowitz after his heavyweight Doug Jones loses a big one.

'I'll put Smokey Joe Frazier into orbit as the first black astronaut!'
Muhammad Ali before his first, losing fight, with Joe Frazier in 1971.

'I'll make Liston think he's fighting ten guys. I'll make him so dizzy he'll think he's on a carousel!'
Muhammad Ali before taking the heavyweight title from Sonny Liston in 1964.

'I'm going to come out smoking!'
Joe Frazier, 1972.

'I'm going to eat hamburgers and cheeseburgers. I'm going to belly bump him all over the ring!'
A bulky George Foreman before losing on points to Evander Holyfield in 1991.

'I'd like to get a steamroller and lay Norton down and crush him flat. Other than that I like him!'

> *George Foreman before his second contest with Ken Norton in 1974.*

'The next time we fight I'm going to knock the "a" out of him and he'll be Sad Muhammad!'

> *Dwight Braxton after beating Matthew Saad Muhammad in 10 rounds in 1981.*

'I'll open up the graveyard and bury his body!'

> *Joe Frazier refuses to be reconciled with old opponent Muhammad Ali.*

'I'll be punching Sanchez to the body, the liver and the heart. If it goes over 10 rounds Sanchez will never be able to fight again!'

> *Wilfredo Gomez before taking a beating from Salvador Sanchez in 1981.*

'He's going to need an industrial strength toothpick to pick the leather out of his teeth. I'm gonna hit this man so hard he's going to grow an Afro!'

> *Michael Olajide shortly before losing to Iran Barkley in five rounds in 1988.*

'I'm going to gut him like a fish. He's just a tomato can!'

> *The once-feared Mike Tyson before losing to Kevin McBride in 2005.*

'I can lick any son-of-a-bitch in the house!'

> *Customary greeting from world heavyweight champion John L. Sullivan upon entering a saloon.*

Pass the Hat Round

In 1913, tough American Frank Klaus was in Paris preparing for his middleweight championship unification bout against Billy Papke. Klaus was accompanied by his manager, George Engel, a doughty former professional fighter himself. Both men stayed at an expensive hotel in the French capital. One night Klaus and Engel had a dispute and started fighting fiercely. The ferocious contest ranged all over the hotel and ended in the lobby after the fighting men had fallen down a flight of stairs. The boxer and his manager fully expected to be ejected ignominiously from the hotel. Instead, the appreciative management and guests passed round the hat and rewarded the Americans with a bundle of money for providing such an entertaining scrap.

Six Heads

Andrew 'Six Heads' Lewis was a very competent welterweight and light middleweight from Guyana who held the WBA welterweight title for a time. However, he is remembered in boxing folklore for two unusual incidents in his career. As an amateur he knocked out an opponent. Back in the dressing room the examining doctor asked the stricken boxer what he could see. The fighter indicated Lewis, who was standing in the background. 'I see six heads!' he gasped. That took care of Lewis's nickname for the rest of his fighting career.

Years later, in Georgetown, Guyana, Lewis was well on top entering the sixth round of a contest against Denny Dalton for the Guyanese light middleweight championship. Suddenly Lewis turned, hurtled through the ropes and sprinted up the aisle to the dressing rooms. Later he said that he had drunk a dodgy milkshake that afternoon and in the ring had experienced an overwhelming desire to go to the toilet. This left the referee the conundrum of whether to disqualify Lewis, announce that he had retired hurt, or declare a 'no contest' decision. He settled for retirement.

An Actor's Life for Me! 4 – Ken Norton

Ken Norton did not learn to box until he was 23 and serving in the Marines. He went on to become a leading heavyweight. In 1974 he was knocked out by George Foreman in a fight for the latter's world title. Leon Spinks took the championship from Ali in only his eighth fight and was ordered to defend it against Norton. Spinks refused, preferring a much more lucrative return bout with Ali. The World Boxing Council stripped Spinks of his championship and awarded it to Norton. Norton defended his new title against Larry Holmes and lost narrowly on points. He entered boxing trivia history as the only heavyweight champion never to have won a title fight. After 42 contests he used his magnificent physique to good effect by gaining a part in the steamy 1975 movie *Madingo,* as a slave who had an affair with a white woman. The role was not quite as satisfying as he might have hoped, because he was quoted as complaining of his role, 'Susan George seduces me. But after you get seduced 12 hours a day, two days straight, it's kinda hard to like it!' Norton made about 20 movies before suffering bad injuries in a car accident.

Diamonds are not Necessarily Forever

Cockney fighter Pedlar Palmer was very proud when he won the world bantamweight championship in 1895. He was even prouder when his supporters clubbed together to buy him a diamond-studded belt valued at £1,000. Generously he would lend his belt to anyone who wanted to examine it. Years later, when he had fallen upon hard times, he took it to be valued. He was told that the belt was practically worthless. Over the years his 'friends' had extracted the diamonds, sold them and replaced them with glass baubles. Or so the story went. However, in 1993 a diamond-encrusted belt was found in the vaults of a Brighton bank. Rumours spread that it was Palmer's belt – completely intact and very valuable.

Assists

Few boxers have been too proud to accept advice when it has been offered, no matter however unlikely the source. Before the Second World War, Benjamin 'Evil Eye' Finkle earned a lucrative living by placing a 'hex' on certain boxers. He claimed that he was able to cause a fighter to lose by the exercise of supernatural powers. A lot of people in the fight game believed him as well. Those who did not still often went along with the act for the sake of the ensuing publicity.

Finkle, an unsuccessful fighter and manager, claimed to have discovered his powers inadvertently when he had glowered balefully at the opponent of one of his fighters. According to the manager the fighter concerned had turned green, started sweating profusely and then performed so ineptly that he had lost a contest he had been in the process of winning. In 1926, Finkle proudly announced his newly discovered ability to the American press. He garnered a great deal of newspaper space in this way. Managers began to slip Finkle a few dollars to place the evil eye on their fighters' opponents, figuring that the expenditure of a small sum could do their boxers no harm. Over the years Finkle was hired to glare menacingly at such champions as Jack Dempsey, Billy Conn and Willy Pastrano. He would explain to anyone who was interested that it made a pleasant change from his day job of selling a bridge over the Mississippi to drunks.

In 1996, Irish super middleweight Steve Collins claimed to have received the help of a hypnotist in his preparations for his WBO championship match with the favourite Chris Eubank. Collins assured the press – and his opponent – that his body had been programmed to deliver twice as many punches as Eubank could deliver. The normally brash and self-confident Eubank protested that the other fighter was taking an unfair advantage over him. At the weigh-in, within earshot of Eubank, the hypnotist told everyone, 'When Eubank hits him I've ensured that Collins will not feel any pain. He'll find Eubank very easy to hit.' Later, Collins admitted that it had all been ballyhoo, but he still won the fight.

Some boxers have lucked out thanks to handicaps sustained by their opponents. In 1910, Welsh featherweight Jim Driscoll was fighting Spike Robson from North Shields at the National Sporting Club in London. At the start of the fifth round, Robson raced across the ring. Driscoll's trainer was about to lift the heavy wooden corner stool over the ropes out of the ring. Robson hurtled into the stool and suffered a severe gash to his face. He insisted on fighting on but he was in a daze for the rest of the bout and was knocked out by Driscoll in the twelfth round.

A quarter of a century later, Tony Canzoneri was a little more fortunate when he encountered Jimmy McLarnin in a bout at Madison Square Garden in 1936. The referee had finished giving both men their pre-fight instructions. Canzoneri turned to trot back to his corner to wait for the opening bell. Instead he walked straight into the hanging microphone used for the announcements. Canzoneri received such a bad cut on his forehead that it later took twelve stitches to close it. When he staggered back to his corner his seconds only had time to wipe some of the blood away. Still in a state of shock the boxer lost the opening round but recovered sufficiently to outpoint McLarnin.

RING NICKNAMES

Here are some of the more curious nicknames fighters have gone by over the years:

Benny 'Little Fish' Bass
Jack 'the Giant Killer' Dillon
Harry 'the Human Hairpin' Harris
Sammy 'the Rockford Sheikh' Mandell
Barry 'the Clones Cyclone' McGuigan
Bobby 'Boogaloo' Watts
Evander 'the Real Deal' Holyfield
Bobby 'No Dice' Chacon
Roberto 'Hands of Stone' Durán
Thomas 'the Hitman' Hearns
Bernard 'the Executioner' Hopkins
Ray 'Boom Boom' Mancini
Lance 'Goofi' Whittaker

James 'Lights Out' Toney
Alfred 'Ice' Cole
Mitch 'Blood' Green
Willie 'the Worm' Monroe
Iran 'the Blade' Barkley
Aaron 'the Hawk' Pryor
James 'Bonecrusher' Smith
Michael 'Second to' Nunn
Mike 'the Bounty' Hunter
DaVarryl 'Touch of Sleep' Williamson
Darnell 'Ding-a-Ling-Man' Wilson

PUT YOUR TRUST IN THE LORD – BUT TRAIN HARD

Heavyweight Con O'Kelly Jnr had 74 bouts in Britain and the USA, of which he won 51. He was then ordained as a Catholic priest. One night he was acting as a second in a boxing tournament for a Stockport boys' club, against a Liverpool team. A Liverpool boy in the opposite corner crossed himself before the start of a bout. 'Will that do him any good, Father?' asked the anxious Stockport boy. 'Not if he hasn't done any training,' said the priest reassuringly.

FIGHT FILMS – THE WORST: 3 – *THE LEATHER SAINT* (1957)

Director: Alvin Ganzer **Screenplay:** Norman Retchin
Leading Players: John Derek, Paul Douglas, César Romero, Jody Lawrance
An Episcopalian minister, and much too pretty to be a fighter, Gil Allen (Derek) boxes anonymously as a professional in order to earn enough money to buy an iron lung and a swimming pool for the underprivileged of his

parish. Because he is otherwise engaged on Sundays he can only train on Saturdays, the days of his fights. He is pursued by an alluring but alcoholic woman, who does not know that he is a minister. Because he does not want to hurt his opponents unnecessarily, the minister will only hit them with one punch – his Sunday punch. He achieves his aim and gives up boxing. Presumably he then has to clean out the pool every week.

FOUL! 4 – MIKE TYSON

When veterans Mike Tyson and Evander Holyfield met for the heavyweight title at Las Vegas in June 1997 nobody expected a pretty fight. What happened, however, attracted headlines all over the world. In the second round, Holyfield opened a cut over Tyson's eye which the latter claimed was caused by a deliberate head-butt. With 40 seconds left in the third round, Tyson worked his opponent into a corner, pinned his arms to his sides and bit Holyfield's right ear. Referee Mills Lane was out of position and did not see what had occurred. He discussed the situation with the Nevada State Boxing Commissioner and deducted two points from Tyson's score.

In the next round an infuriated Tyson bit Holyfield's other ear. This time Lane stepped in and disqualified the half-crazed heavyweight. 'That's it, Mike,' he said. 'You're outta here. You're done!' Afterwards Tyson mused, 'My greatest weakness is my sensitivity.'

RINGWISE

The first bare-knuckle prize fights were held in open fields in roughly marked-out spaces. A scratched circle for the fighters was given the name 'ring'. Roped squares were in use by 1838. After the introduction of the Marquess of Queensberry Rules to regulate the sport, padded rings were introduced towards the end of the nineteenth century. The bare-knuckle rings were between 20ft and 24ft square. Modern professional rings are between 16ft and 20ft square. They are set on raised platforms, with a post at each corner, and four ropes.

In the second round of a bout between Sugar Ray Leonard and Roberto Durán in New Orleans in 1980, the ring suddenly collapsed. The promoter had recruited sixteen college footballers to act as security guards. He ordered them under the ring to make running repairs and then to remain crouching there supporting the canvas on their shoulders. Durán retired in the eighth round. There is some confusion as to whether Durán actually uttered his notorious phrase 'No mas. No mas box' ('No more. No more boxing'), or whether the statement was coined by commentator Howard Cossell.

FIGHT FILMS – THE BEST: 4 – *ROCKY* (1970)

Director: John G. Avildsen **Screenplay:** Sylvester Stallone
Leading Players: Sylvester Stallone, Talia Shire, Burt Young, Carl Weathers, Burgess Meredith
Stallone's screenplay of the Cinderella theme played against a Philadelphia boxing background owed its inception to the 1975 Muhammad Ali–Chuck Wepner fight in which

veteran Wepner, 'the Bayonne Bleeder', showed enormous courage against the champion and even knocked Ali off his feet momentarily before being beaten in the 15th round. Stallone wrote a script in which a surprisingly sensitive journeyman fighter is given a chance in a million to fight for the world heavyweight title. In the process his life is changed beyond recognition and he puts up a tremendous fight to take the champion, played by former pro-footballer Carl Weathers, to a split decision.

The role of the champion was originally meant for professional heavyweight Ken Norton. Joe Frazier has a walk-on as himself.

Stallone insisted on playing the title role himself and turned in a masterly depiction of an underdog who found love and self-respect as his character developed against incredible odds.

The championship bout is outstandingly done although the sound effects are perhaps a little overdone, with many of the punches sounding as if a car door is being slammed.

The first screenplay was written in three days but there were many revisions. In one draft Rocky was even going to throw the fight! Stallone choreographed the fight sequence himself, basing it on the Rocky Marciano–Ezzard Charles championship bouts. He was Oscar-nominated for both his performance and screenplay.

GET THE WORDS RIGHT

Singer Robert Goulet was offered two ringside tickets if he would sing the American national anthem before the one-round debacle of the second Ali–Liston fight at Lewiston, Maine, in 1965. He practised the words all day. When the big moment came he made a mistake. Instead of singing 'Oh, say can you see by the dawn's early light,' Goulet ended the line with the word 'night'. This caused an uproar and damaged his professional reputation for a while. Afterwards he said bitterly, 'I said one word wrong. The fight lasted a minute and a half and they blamed me!'

'I Know when I've had Enough!'

'. . . Private Clohessy (Munster Fusiliers) lasted the three rounds in the final, only to lose on points. I met Clohessy again in the final round of another competition at Lucknow in February, 1910, when he gave in after two and a half rounds, and as he ran up against me at Lahore shortly afterwards, in yet one more final, he declined to box on the grounds that it wasn't much use.'

Bombardier Billy Wells, British Heavyweight Champion (1911–19) discusses his early boxing days in the army in India.

Telegenic

By the end of the 1950s boxing was very popular on US television. Weekly shows attracted large audiences. Pabst Blue Ribbon Beer sponsored Wednesday night tournaments while Friday night shows were backed by Gillette. Managers vied with one another to get their fighters a lucrative televised spot. One promoter, Harry Glickman, could not understand why a competent yet undistinguished middleweight called Ralph 'Tiger' Jones got so many television engagements. He appeared in at least 50 bouts on the box. Finally, someone inside the media tipped Glickman the wink. Jones had a great chin but no punch. This meant that most of his bouts travelled the full distance, giving the television companies time to air their full quota of commercials and keeping their sponsors satisfied.

OSCAR BONAVENA

For a time, Argentinian Oscar Bonavena was a leading contender for the World Heavyweight title. He defeated Zora Folley and George Chuvalo and lasted as far as the 15th round before being stopped by Muhammad Ali.

Outside the ring he proved more vulnerable. One day in 1976, he stormed into the Mustang Ranch, a legalised brothel near Reno. Bonavena was looking for the owner, with whom he had a dispute. Instead he was confronted by one of the owner's henchmen. The man took no chances. He shot the heavyweight in the chest with a rifle and killed him.

ROCKY AND THE WELSHMAN

Rocky Marciano was the heavyweight champion of the world from 1952 until his retirement in 1956. He was undefeated as a professional, winning 49 fights, 43 of them inside the distance. Yet when he was a young soldier stationed in Wales in the Second World War, he was taken the full distance by a medical student.

As a 19-year-old GI, Marciano was stationed at St Athans with the 150th Combat Engineers. One night a team boxing contest was arranged between the American troops in the area and a side of medical students from Cardiff University. Marciano's opponent was a 22-year-old rugby player Jack Matthews. Matthews had been given a trial for Wales in the centre in 1939, but the war had put an end to international rugby. When Matthews entered the ring he was told that his opponent had won his last six contests by knockouts. 'I'm not going to be the bloody seventh,' he replied grimly.

Matthews took the future world champion the full three rounds. 'When the final bell went I was quite pleased,' he later said mildly. No decision was given. After the war Matthews became a doctor, played rugby for Cardiff and Newport, was awarded 17 Welsh caps and toured with the British Lions.

The Champion who Started a Mutiny

Harry Reeve was briefly the British light heavyweight champion between 1916 and 1917. A tough Stepney fighter, over the course of his career he met world champions Battling Siki and Mike McTigue and more than a dozen British title-holders. But the incident for which Reeve was to be best remembered was the fact that he sparked off the most notorious mutiny in the British Army in the First World War.

After a spell as a physical training instructor, Reeve was posted to France as a military policeman at the dreaded base-camp of Etaples. This was a hell-hole where British and Commonwealth troops were sent for retraining behind the lines. The staff members at the camp were known to be vicious bullies. Discipline was savage and long hours were spent in merciless drill, conducted at the double.

By the time that Reeve arrived, the camp was close to mutiny. Matters came to a head on Sunday 9 September and the unfortunate Reeve was soon in the thick of the action. A large crowd of British, Australian and New Zealand troops had gathered outside the guardhouse to protest at the arrest of a New Zealand gunner.

Private Harry Reeve was the first member of the staff to attempt to move on the hundreds of milling men. In order to do this he pushed an Australian, who refused to be moved. The angry champion then struck the Australian several times with his fist. This caused an uproar among the other soldiers, who closed in ominously on Reeve, lashing out at the military policeman.

The panic-stricken Reeve seized a revolver from one of the men in the mob and, he claimed, fired several warning shots in the air. One of these shots hit and wounded a French woman standing some way off. A second shot killed a Corporal W.B. Wood of the Gordon Highlanders, who was passing by innocently on the fringe of the mob.

This action sparked off the mutiny. Furious soldiers turned on all the military policemen and their officers in an uprising that lasted for several days. The camp staff fled for their lives. Most of the soldiers in the camp poured into Etaples and roamed the streets freely. The camp commandant was seized and carried mockingly around the town on the shoulders of jeering troops.

The authorities moved quickly to restore order. Reinforcements were called in and the existing staff transferred out quickly. The commanding officer was hustled off into retirement and most of the mutineers were dispatched to front-line units.

Private Harry Reeve was court-martialled for the manslaughter of Corporal Wood. He was sentenced to a year's hard labour. Upon his release he was sent to the front for the Allied final 'Big Push' of 1918. His leg was badly damaged by shrapnel and he spent months in a military hospital.

After the war Reeve tried to resume his boxing career but his damaged calf meant that he could never move easily again. He took part in many more fights, because boxing was the only trade he had, but he was now fighting at the bottom of the bill for small purses.

He continued in the ring until 1928, retired for six years and then tried a comeback at the age of 41. After a handful of bouts he called it a day and became a stevedore on the docks. He died in 1958 at the age of 65.

Weight Gain

In 1955, light heavyweight Peter Aldridge was given the chance of a top-of-the bill fight in Newcastle against Scottish heavyweight champion Hugh Fearns for a purse of £280. Aldridge wanted the money but he knew that the British Boxing Board of Control would not sanction the match because he would be giving away 42lb in weight. Aldridge's manager, former British Heavyweight Champion Bruce Woodcock, came up with a cunning plan. At the weigh-in before the bout, Aldridge stood on the scales with a lead window sash weighing a stone secreted beneath his shorts. This gave him an extra 14lb in weight. A sharp-eyed reporter noticed that Aldridge was moving awkwardly and asked if something was wrong with his legs. 'He's just stiff from the long train journey,' Woodcock assured him. The Board allowed the fight to continue. Having removed the sash Aldridge went on to box a draw with Fearns and earn his money.

THE GREAT CHAMPIONS:
5 – SUGAR RAY ROBINSON: 1921–89

Main weights: welterweight, middleweight
Contests: 200 **Won:** 173 (KO: 108) **Lost:** 19 **Drew:** 6

Many have rated 'Sugar' Ray Robinson the best all-round boxer ever. He had speed of hand, great co-ordination and skill. Over a 25-year ring career he held the world welterweight title for 5 years, was 5 times middleweight champion and came close to winning the light heavyweight championship. As a boy in Detroit he carried heavyweight champion Joe Louis's equipment to the gym for him. He was undefeated in 85 amateur contests, winning several Golden Gloves titles. He turned professional in 1940 and won 26 consecutive bouts in his first year. In his 41st professional fight he lost to the experienced Jake LaMotta. Robinson had just received his draft notice and was distracted. He won the vacant world welterweight championship, giving this up when he had won the middleweight championship from LaMotta, a fighter he was to defeat a total of four times. Robinson remained undefeated for eight years before embarking on a tour of Europe to participate in half a dozen bouts. A sign that he did not take this trip too seriously was evinced by the size of his entourage. With Robinson went his manager, trainer, golf professional, secretary, hairdresser, a dwarf, his wife and his sister and 100 pieces of baggage.

In London Robinson lost his middleweight championship to Randolph Turpin. He regained it on a stoppage in New York 64 days later. He tried to take the light heavyweight title from Joey Maxim during a heat wave in New York but collapsed from dehydration. This caused Maxim to ask caustically, 'What did they think I had in my corner – air conditioning?' Robinson retired but made a number of comebacks, briefly regaining his championship. He retired for the last time in 1965 at the age of 44.

Planning a Career

'The purses which were given in England in those days were far too small and infrequent to enable any professional boxer to make both a decent livelihood and to save money for his old age, so that, unless a man was willing to attach himself to a booth or to spar nightly at the sporting houses, he either had to find a "governor" or to follow some regular occupation, at the risk of becoming muscle-bound through hard labour, and of thereby losing his form.'

Jim Driscoll, featherweight champion of Great Britain,
writing in 1914.

An Actor's Life for Me!
5 – Lennox Lewis and Wladimir Klitschko

Lennox Lewis and Wladimir Klitschko played boxers due to meet in the crime caper movie *Oceans 11* (2001). No one knew the eventual result because as part of a robbery scam all the lights went out in the casino where the bout was taking place. In real life, Lewis lost his next fight, to Hasim Rahman, which he blamed on the distractions of filming. Later he beat Klitschko in real fight, stopping him with a badly cut eye in the sixth round.

THE GREAT CHAMPIONS:
6 – JACK DEMPSEY: 1895–1983

Main weight: heavyweight **Contests:** 83 **Won:** 66 (KO:51) **Lost:** 6 **Drew:** 11

'The Manassa Mauler', one of 11 children and a former hobo who rode the rails and fought merely for hand outs in the saloons and mining camps of the Western states, Dempsey revolutionised boxing with his wild free-swinging style, solid chin and utter fearlessness. He would chew resin to strengten his jaw and soak his hands in brine to toughen them. Dempsey was fortunate to fall in with one of the outstanding and shrewdest managers of the day, Jack 'Doc' Kearns. Kearns brought Dempsey along carefully and when the fighter was ready he let him loose on the leading white heavyweights, although he guided Dempsey away from the dangerous black fighters of the day like Sam Langford. In 1918, Dempsey knocked out 17 opponents, 12 of them in the first round. By 1919 Dempsey had blasted out Fireman Jim Flynn, Gunboat Smith and Carl Morris.

On 4 July 1919, Dempsey took the title from the mountainous Jess Willard, breaking the champion's jaw in the process and flooring him seven times. At first Dempsey was not a popular champion as he had avoided war service, but his whole-hearted style and expansive personality gradually won the fans over. Over a seven-year reign he defended his title only five times, but each bout drew huge crowds. He knocked out Billy Miske and Bill Brennan and an international contest against Frenchman Georges Carpentier drew the first million-dollar gate. He outpointed Tommy Gibbons and then recovered from being knocked out of the ring to clamber back in and knock out Argentinian Luis Ángel Firpo in the second round.

He earned good money in exhibition bouts and vaudeville and stage appearances. In 1926, he lost his title to the cerebral 'Fighting Marine' Gene Tunney. He tried again the following year but although he knocked the new champion down for what seemed like an extended count, Tunney recovered to retain his championship on a points decision.

For the rest of his long life, Dempsey opened a popular New York restaurant, made personal appearances and refereed contests, sometimes earning up to $10,000 a night, even during the Depression.

AN ACTOR'S LIFE FOR ME! 6 – EARNIE SHAVERS

Not every boxer who tried to break into the movies made it. Earnie Shavers was one of the most fearsome-looking and hardest-punching heavyweights of the 1970s. When he heard that Sylvester Stallone was looking for a villainous-looking character to play the awesome Clubber Lang in *Rocky III,* Shavers turned up for the auditions with hope in his heart. However, in a fight scene he hit the star so hard that when Stallone came round he told his opponent that he had failed the test, because the public would never accept the fact that Stallone could defeat Shavers.

MEN OF THE CLOTH: 2 –TOMMY BURNS

Canadian Tommy Burns (1881–1955), born Noah Brusso, won the World Heavyweight championship when he defeated Marvin Hart in 1906. Burns, at a height of 5ft 7in, was the smallest man ever to win the title. He was, however, a shrewd businessman and adept at winding up his opponents, which enabled him to make money from boxing and defeat a number of challengers for his title. He beat Fireman Jim Flynn and Bill Squires and then conducted a successful whistle-stop tour of Europe, defeating Gunner Moir, Jack Palmer, Jem Roche and Jewey Smith.

Cashing in on his title, Burns then travelled to Australia and beat the best of their big men. Ultimately, however, he came up against his nemesis in Jack Johnson, the big black fighter who had stalked the title-holder, issuing challenges, across the world. The two men finally met at Rushcutter's Bay, outside Sydney, on Boxing Day 1908. Burns received a record-breaking $30,000 for defending his title, but although he fought bravely he was defeated in the 14th round, when the police intervened to stop the slaughter.

Burns fought on for a while but then retired and devoted himself to a number of occupations. He became a boxing manager and promoter, ran a men's clothing store in Calgary, served as a physical training instructor in the Canadian Army in the First World War, ran a pub in Newcastle in England and opened a speakeasy in New York. He lost most of his savings during the Wall Street Crash of 1929 and drifted around for a considerable time after that.

He had always been a churchgoer and in 1948 he was ordained as a minister of the Church on Christmas Day. He travelled up and down California, conducting evangelistic meetings. He worked in orphanages, hospitals and prisons.

He died in Vancouver in 1955 at the age of 73. Burns had been visiting a friend, John Westaway, who led an evangelical church called the Temple of Christ Healing. Burns collapsed and died after a heart attack. After his death it was discovered that he had no money left and he was buried in a paupers' grave. Two gravediggers and two passers-by were in attendance at his funeral.

FOUL! 5 – FELTON AND SCHNEIDER

Probably the quickest double-disqualification on record occurred in Maryland in 2008. Heavyweights Jonathan Felton and Askia Schneider got into a dispute as soon as they entered the ring. They started hitting each other and were both disqualified before the bell sounded to start the fight.

A GREEN FIGHTER?

Stephen Strong was a well-known bare-knuckle fighter in the Bristol region, particularly after he had adopted the ring name of Iron Arm Cabbage. The origins of the sobriquet are unknown; perhaps Strong picked cabbages in the fields around Hanham, his home village. One day, Cabbage challenged and defeated a touring booth fighter and was spotted by the English champion Tom Cribb. Cribb was impressed by what he saw but counselled Cabbage to remain in the West Country gathering experience before challenging more experienced fighters.

However, Cabbage was an impetuous youth. He defeated a Bristol fighter called Abe Newton and then, as a contemporary newspaper recounted, decided to challenge the world. 'Nothing would satisfy Mr Cabbage and his friends but going up to London and proving to the Cockneys that the Bristol School could still turn out boxers . . . But they flew too high at the game when they matched the Cabbage against Jack Martin, the Master of the Rolls (a baker), then at his very best.' Cabbage lost to Martin and then became distracted by the fleshpots of London. As another newspaper put it, 'Cabbage was a difficult man to train, for if there was a petticoat or a pint of beer within reach he was bound to go for it.'

Cabbage fought on for a time but after being beaten badly by Gypsy Cooper he abandoned the ring and his name and returned to West Country life as Mr Stephen Strong.

Take Your Best Shot!

Theodore 'Tiger' Flowers was one of the best middleweights in the world in the 1920s, and in 1926 he was to win the world title. However, because he was black he was accustomed to having to take it easy with white opponents in order to get fights. One evening in December 1925 he was matched in Boston against a touring Welsh fighter, Frank Moody. Almost out of habit, Flowers sent word to Moody's dressing room that he was prepared to coast against the Welshman. The affronted Moody, who never took a backwards step, replied that he did not need Flowers' charity and that the American was to fight all-out. This turned out to be a big mistake. The unleashed Flowers gave Moody a tremendous thrashing over the ten rounds' distance.

Triple-Hitters

Some contests have been so terrific that a return match was a necessity. Sometimes boxers have met more than twice. Two of the great triple-hitters in the heavyweight division have been the bouts between Floyd Patterson and Ingemar Johansson, and the Muhammad Ali–Joe Frazier trilogy.

Floyd Patterson v. Ingemar Johansson

When Floyd Patterson defended his world heavyweight championship against the European title holder, the Swede Ingemar Johansson, he expected an easy ride, but Johansson displayed a mighty right-hand match to take Patterson's world crown and set up two thrilling return matches:

June, 1959: Yankee Stadium. After two quiet rounds, Johansson suddenly unleashed the mighty right-hand that he called 'the Hammer of Thor'. It smashed Patterson to the canvas. Gamely he got up, but was knocked down six more times. Patterson was so fuddled that he actually thought that he was ahead on points. The referee stopped the bout in the third round, with the champion unable to defend himself. 'Losing the world title was bad enough,' confessed a groggy Patterson. 'Losing it to a foreigner was even worse.'

June, 1960: Polo Grounds, New York. Johansson did not train well for the return bout, while Patterson dedicated himself to getting into condition. Again the Swede started well, stunning Patterson with a right in the second round, but Patterson did not go down. Gaining in confidence, Patterson started to punish the champion. In the fifth round he knocked Johansson down for a count of nine. When the champion rose, Patterson knocked him out with a series of left hooks.

March, 1961:Convention Hall, Miami Beach. Again the playboy Johansson neglected his training. Even so, he floored Patterson in the opening round with a right and when his opponent rose put him down again, this time with a left. Johansson charged in for the kill, only to be knocked down by Patterson. In the second round the two heavyweights stood toe-to-toe, exchanging heavy punches. Patterson began to get on top over the next three rounds as his opponent's lack of conditioning began to tell. In the sixth round Johansson forced Patterson back, but the champion knocked him out with a left hook, to end one of the most thrilling of all heavyweight championship series.

Muhammad Ali v. Joe Frazier
March, 1971: Madison Square Garden, New York. When the charismatic Ali was stripped of his title for refusing to be drafted, Joe Frazier came through a series of elimination contests as the new champion. When Ali emerged from a three-year period of exile, he and Frazier were matched, with each fighter guaranteed $2.5 million. Ali was 29 and Frazier was three years younger. Frazier was the official champion but Ali called himself the 'People's Champion'.

From the opening bell Ali tried to keep his shorter opponent at bay but Frazier kept boring forward. Increasingly Ali was being forced to the ropes, but although he was landing more punches than Frazier, the latter was hitting harder and Ali was being forced to stand toe-to-toe with the other man. In the 9th round Ali made a real effort to get up on his toes and box. Frazier continued to bull his way into the action, slamming away to the body. In the 15th and final round Frazier got through with a left hook and sent Ali spinning to the canvas for a short count. The referee scored the fight 8 rounds to Frazier, 6 to Ali and 1 even. One judge scored it 9–6 and the other 11–4 to Frazier. The victor was so exhausted he had to spend three weeks recovering in hospital afterwards.

January, 1974: Madison Square Garden, New York. Three years passed before the two men met again. By this time Joe Frazier had lost his title in an upset knockout decision to George Foreman. Their second bout was a gruelling 12 round one. By now Ali had thrown off all his ring rust and he boxed superbly throughout. In the second round he hit Frazier with a straight right that staggered the other man. Frazier came back and stunned Ali in the 7th round, but Ali went back to his boxing. He outpointed Frazier by a unanimous decision.

October, 1975: Philippine Coliseum, Quezon City, Manila. The 'Thriller in Manila' is considered one of the greatest of all heavyweight championship contests. This time Ali abandoned all thought of dancing round his opponent. From the opening bell he stood flat-footed in the centre of the ring. He took the opening rounds but in the 4th, 5th and 6th Frazier punched his way back into contention. By the 10th round there was very little in it. In the 12th and 13th rounds Ali took over again, punishing his game opponent with heavy punches and combinations. Ali kept on top during the 14th round and in the interval before the start of the 15th, Frazier's corner retired their exhausted man. After the bout, a shattered Ali said that the experience had been the closest he had ever come to death.

FIGHT FILMS – THE WORST:
4 – *EXCUSE MY GLOVE* (1936)

Director Redd Davis **Screenplay:** Val Valentine and Katherine Strueby **Leading Players:** Len Harvey, Olive Blakeney, Bobbie Comber

This is a cheapo British quota quickie, with all that that implies – wooden acting, leaden direction and unconvincing sets. Len Harvey, variously British middleweight, light heavyweight and heavyweight champion plays, unconvincingly, a mild collector of fine glass who is inveigled into boxing at a fun fair and displays unexpected fistic talent. This is exploited by a booth proprietor who launches the collector onto an unhappy and danger-strewn professional career.

What the film does have going for it for fight fans is a collection of minor non-performances by some of the leading British boxers of the twentieth century. They include heavyweight champions Bombardier Billy Wells, Tommy Farr and Gunner Moir, world flyweight champion Jimmy Wilde and leading contenders Andre Lenglet, Don McCorkindale and Dave McCleve.

CALL ME CHAMP!

Hector Constance was a good have-gloves-will-travel welterweight journeyman from the West Indies. Between 1948 and 1969 he had 87 fights and performed in Great Britain, the USA, Italy, Germany, Turkey, Spain and a number of other countries.

He won 34 of his contests but one defeat that he did endure came in the Chancery Division of the High Court in London. Upon his arrival in England, in order to boost his chances of employment Constance had claimed to be the welterweight champion of Trinidad and the West Indies, and had included these titles on his billing matter. As the boxer later admitted, he did not even know that there were welterweight championships of these areas.

Unfortunately for Constance, the genuine holder of these titles took exception to his usurping them. Hugh Serville had won the championships three months after Constance had left to pursue his career in Europe. In fact, back home in the West Indies Constance had defeated Serville, but not for the titles. Constance's barrister tried to emphasise the essentially transient nature of Serville's claims: 'A boxing champion was here today and gone tomorrow. Being a champion was not inherent in Serville or his boxing career. Two minutes in the ring might easily see the end of it.'

The judge was plainly impressed by Constance's ready admission that he had claimed to be a champion merely to enhance his chances of getting work. As soon as Serville had complained, Constance had announced his readiness to admit that he was not the champion and to give an undertaking not to claim the championship again, unless he were to win it in the ring. Hugh Serville was ordered to pay the costs of the case.

Foul! 6 – Arthur Chambers

In 1872, Arthur Chambers took a sustained beating on Squirrel Island in Canada at the hands of his opponent Billy Edwards. When he came out for the 26th round, Chambers suddenly collapsed, screaming that Edwards had bitten him. The referee saw that there was indeed a fresh bite mark on the fighter's shoulder. He disqualified Edwards and awarded the decision to Chambers. Later it was rumoured that, in an effort to save the fight, Chambers' second had bitten him just before his man left the corner for Round 26.

A Good Marriage

Handsome Enzo Fiermonte was a very good Italian middleweight boxer with a record of 43 victories in 56 fights in Italy, South America and the USA. Some thought that his looks were wasted on a boxer. Fiermonte might have shared that opinion because he gave up the ring to become a film actor. In 1933, after a whirlwind courtship he married Madeleine Astor, the widow of the fabulously wealthy John Jacob Astor IV. They were divorced five years later but Fiermonte went on to appear in more than a hundred movies before his death in 1993.

Sore Loser

In 1912, Abe Attell lost his world featherweight championship to Johnny Kilbane on points over 20 rounds. It was a boring, foul-filled fight. Attell thumbed, butted and hit his opponent low. Kilbane stood off and would not make a fight of it. Afterwards, Kilbane accused Attell of having chloroform smeared on his back, so that the fumes would daze his opponent. Attell denied the charge, claiming that the substance on his back was cocoa butter, designed to cool him down. For years Kilbane repeated his accusation and Attell continued to resent it. When they were both middle-aged they met again at a sports function. Attell threatened to punch Kilbane on the nose. Kilbane laughed and walked away.

Back to the Drawing Board

Boxing promoters have often sought the sport's holy grail of finding and developing their own future world heavyweight champion. In 1985, two Leicester promoters started their campaign by placing an advertisement in the trade newspaper *Boxing News*. They offered a prize of £20,000 to any novice heavyweight who could win his first ten fights at Leicester's Granby Hall. The stipulations were that the successful candidate should weigh over 14 and a half stone and be in the region of 6ft 3in tall.

More than 40 applicants were put through their paces in a gymnasium. The selected candidate was 19-year-old David Shelton, a labourer. Mr Shelton lost three out of four fights, two of them in the first round, before vanishing from the boxing record books.

Sing Up!

At the 1960 Rome Olympics, US Army Sergeant Eddie Crook went up to receive his gold medal. The crowd had not liked his deliberate, calculating style and started booing and hissing. An American sitting in the audience stood up and in response to the booing led all the other Americans in the hall in singing 'The Star Spangled Banner'. The singer was Bing Crosby, the film star crooner. Crook went on to serve with distinction as a sergeant major in Vietnam, winning a Silver Star, Bronze Star and two Purple Hearts.

Referee for Hire

Teddy Brenner went on to work as a well-known American boxing matchmaker. Quite early in his career he was introduced to the less savoury side of professional boxing. In 1938 he was working as a second at a New Jersey tournament. Before the contest between Eddie Alzek and Freddie Cochrane could get under way the referee walked to both corners and asked the fighters how much they would pay him to give the decision in their favour. Neither boxer could afford to pay him anything. At once the referee lost all interest in the bout and at the end declared the result to be a draw.

The Solitary Samoan

Maselino Masoe, based in New Zealand, had over 30 fights as a professional. In 2004 he won the WBA version of the world middleweight championship, losing it upon his first defence two years later. His main claim to fame, however, was that he was the only Samoan ever to win a world boxing title.

Death of a Sparring Partner

Sergeant Major Charles Willcox of the 1st Battalion of the Somerset Regiment had a most distinguished record in the First World War. He won the Military Medal, the Croix de Guerre and the Russian Order of St George. He was mentioned in dispatches on five occasions and twice escaped from German prisoner of war camps.

Standing 6ft 4in in height, he was the captain of the Bridgwater Rugby Football Club and also represented Somerset at the sport. Willcox was also an enthusiastic novice amateur boxer. In 1919, he heard that the British Heavyweight Champion Joe Beckett was having difficulty in finding sparring partners to prepare him for a match with the famous Frenchman, Georges Carpentier. Beckett was a tough former fairground boxer with a good left hook. Impelled by nothing other than patriotism, Willcox approached Beckett's manager Bernard Mortimer and offered to spar with the champion for nothing. He just wanted to see Beckett beat Carpentier.

Mortimer and Beckett were concerned by Willcox's lack of professional experience but impressed by his magnificent physique and enthusiasm. They took him on at their Southampton training camp to help out with Beckett's sparring. After a few days they both began to be concerned by the amount of punishment that Willcox was shipping and his refusal to back off from the much more experienced Beckett.

Some way through the training session, Willcox took a day off to enter a novice heavyweight competition at the National Sporting Club. In his first bout he was floored and struck his head heavily on the canvas. Charles Willcox never recovered consciousness.

At the subsequent inquest the matter of the punishment that Willcox had received while sparring with Beckett was raised. The coroner, Mr F. Danford Thomas, wondered whether the earlier heavy blows Willcox had taken from Joe Beckett had caused some form of brain damage which had contributed to his collapse at the NSC. Willcox had talked about the strength of Beckett's punches to other sparring partners. At the inquest, Beckett admitted, 'When I am boxing a man I do not know how hard I hit him, or how I hurt him. I know nothing about what Willcox complained of. He looked to me to be quite well. I was very sorry to hear of his death, very sorry indeed.'

The jury returned a verdict of excusable homicide by misadventure. When Joe Beckett fought Georges Carpentier at Holborn Stadium he was knocked out inside a minute of the opening round.

RING RAGE

When 'Dangerous' Dan Harkness lost his bout at Glasgow in 1938, he was so disgusted that he hit the referee, Norman Dickson, and as a result served a long period of suspension. The following year he made his comeback at Coatbridge and was adjudged the loser against Johnny Slavin. Once again the losing boxer hauled off and floored the referee, Peter Muir. This brought an end to Dangerous Dan's brief but turbulent boxing career.

'LET'S GET READY TO RUMBLE!'

Ring announcer Michael Buffer, grandson of former world flyweight and bantamweight champion Johnny Buff, has been famous for 25 years for his pre-fight howl 'Let's get ready to rumble.' He reckons that it has generated more than $400 million in the sales of video games and other licenced products. It has also secured him roles in a number of movies. He is quick to protect his copyright. He reckons that over the years he has sent out more than 250 'cease-and-desist' lawyers' letters warning others off using his catchphrase.

Sentencing

In 1937, at the London Sessions, the magistrates dealt with a case of a youth found guilty of stealing a motor car. They offered him a choice of going to a Borstal institution or of being bound over if he agreed to learn to box. The accused chose the latter option. An ironic leading article in *The Times* suggested that it would only be a short while before each court had its own resident pugilist hired to teach offenders to box.

Mob Connected

Big Andre Anderson had been considered a promising heavyweight in his early days just before the First World War. He went the distance with Jack Dempsey in a no-decision bout in the latter's first visit to New York and defeated White Hope Al Palzer. He saw active service in Europe during the war but when he returned he fell into the hands of mobsters and became suspected of losing bouts to order. When he was matched against Wayne 'Big Boy' Munn in 1925, Anderson revolted. 'I'm through throwing fights and laying down whenever they want me to,' he declared. 'I'm going to knock Munn out in one punch, if I can.' He was as good as his word, knocking his opponent out in the first round. A few months later, in 1926, Anderson was dead, shot in mysterious circumstances in Cicero, Illinois. It was said that Ernest Hemingway used Anderson as the model for his doomed fighter Ole Anderson, killed by gangsters at the beginning of his 1927 short story *The Killers,* but the author denied this.

The 'African Ball Dodger'

Jobs were hard to come by in the USA for African American athletes in the 1890s. When Bob Allen was offered a job in a Boston circus, he grabbed it. The job was replacing a sick performer known as the 'African Ball Dodger'. It was the dodger's task to avoid hard balls thrown at him by patrons. The nimble Allen proved so adept at this and improved his footwork so considerably that he took up professional boxing and earned a reputation as a good defensive fighter between 1892 and 1909.

The Great Champions: 7 – Archie Moore: 1916–98

Main weight: light heavyweight **Contests:** 220
Won: 185 (KO: 131) **Lost:** 23 **Drew:** 11

For decades Archie Moore was almost too good. He had a wide array of boxing skills, could punch hard and feared no one. But he was an African American and in the 1930s and '40s chances at championships were few and far between. Moore had to tour the world, including a successful trip to Australia, picking up bouts for peanuts where he could find them. He started as a welterweight in 1935 and gradually worked his way through the weight divisions until ending up mixing it with heavyweights towards the end of his career. It was as a light heavyweight, however, that he flourished, and was perhaps one of the best of them all. He fought wherever and whenever he could, picking up and discarding managers along the route. It was a tough apprenticeship, causing him to remark once, 'In this game you have got to be a finisher. I call it "finishing" and you don't learn it in Miss Hewitt's school for young ladies.' In order to get fights he would write to newspapers, stating his claims to a title bout. It was not until 1952 and he was almost 40 that he secured a bout with Joey Maxim for the world light heavyweight title, outpointing his opponent by a wide margin. Moore defended the title for eight years until the NBA took his title away from him after he refused to defend it against Harold Johnson, a man he had already defeated four times (years before, Moore had even beaten Johnson's father). The other governing bodies continued to recognise Moore. He became notorious for his dietary methods, chewing pieces of steak to extract the goodness and then spitting them out. Towards the end of his career, his eyesight was poor. At the weigh-in for his bout against the much younger Willy Pastrano, Moore could not read the eye charts on the wall. He merely shrugged and mumbled, 'Hell, Willy ain't going to be that far away anyhow!' He never lost his light heavyweight belt in the ring. Towards the end of his career he secured lucrative losing bouts against a couple of heavyweight champions in Rocky Marciano (lost in nine) and Floyd Patterson (lost in five). At 21, Patterson was exactly half his opponent's age. Moore even put Marciano on the canvas for a brief count.

Silent Hairston

Gene 'Silent' Hairston was a very useful middleweight of the 1940s and '50s, beating two world champions in Kid Gavilán and Paul Pender. In all of his 63 fights, however, he boxed under a handicap. Silent Hairston was deaf. During fights he had to have lights flashed from the ring corners to indicate that a round was over.

THE GREAT CHAMPIONS:
8 – WILLIE PEP: 1922–2006

Main weight: featherweight **Contests:** 241
Won: 229 (KO:65) **Lost:** 11 **Drew:**1

Known as 'Will o' the Wisp' for his consummate defensive boxing skills, as a boy Willie Pep shined shoes on the streets of his native Middleton in Connecticut. He developed enormous boxing skills, had a good amateur career and turned professional in 1940. His speed and boxing ability together with a readiness to mix it when necessary soon made him a popular top-of-the-bill boxer. In 1942, he won the New York Athletic Association's version of the world featherweight title, although he was only 20. He retained this championship for six years and added the NBA title to his collection in 1946. He served briefly and unhappily in both the army and the navy during the war.

Pep remained undefeated in his first 63 fights. He went on to lose only once in his first 136 contests, being beaten only by the heavier wartime lightweight champion Sammy Angott. In 1947 he suffered a broken leg and several cracked vertebrae in an aircraft crash in New Jersey. After only six months Pep was back in the ring, outpointing Victor Flores without losing a single round.

In 1948, Pep was matched with the tall, heavy-punching Sandy Saddler and lost his title by a 4th-round knockout. Pep regained his championship several months later on a points decision but lost a third, foul-filled contest when he retired in the 8th round. He continued to tour the country fighting all-comers but was beginning to lose his speed and durability. The New York State Athletic Commission withdrew his licence to box in 1954, after he had been stopped in two rounds by Lulu Perez, but Pep was able to carry on fighting in other parts of the USA. He retired for good in 1966 and became a referee and after-dinner speaker, where he regaled his listeners with such wry quips as, 'First your legs go. Then you lose your reflexes. Then you lose your friends.'

BOXING CLICHÉS

experienced – knackered

cagey – unenterprising

journeyman – knackered *and* unenterprising

controversial decision – a bung has gone in

feeling each other out – mutual apprehension

he's got some ground to make up – outclassed

epic encounter – better than the usual rubbish

a good left-hand – only uses his right to scratch his nose

gutsy – thick

doesn't know when he's beaten – extremely thick

playing to the crowd – big-headed extrovert

spectacular entrance – big-headed extrovert who can afford flash gear

going for a quick finish – too unfit to last more than a couple of rounds

dancing round the ring – scuttling like a frightened rabbit

hard man – has never learned to box

knows all the tricks – dirty git

a last-minute substitute – a drunk with a boxing licence who was passing the hall at the wrong time

School of Hard Knocks

Boxing has always attracted hard men. A number of champions and challengers were taught to box while they were banged up in prison or reformatory schools. Among those who've served time are Sonny Liston, Floyd Patterson, Jake LaMotta, Trevor Berbick, Riddick Bowe and Ron Lyle.

One of the first examples of a lockup being used as a finishing school occurred in Galveston, Texas, in 1901. A local fighter, Jack Johnson, future world heavyweight champion, had only had 11 contests but was attracting a lot of interest as a coming man. His backers imported a brilliant Jewish fighter called Joe Choynski to test their protégé.

Choynski was smaller and older than Johnson but much more experienced, with 68 contests. He was regarded as one of the most brilliant fighters of his time.

Choynski proved much too good for his opponent and knocked Johnson out in the third round. Immediately, five armed Texas Rangers stepped into the ring and arrested both participants for taking part in an illegal prize-fight. Johnson and Choynski were taken to the same prison. To while away the idle hours, Choynski gave his erstwhile opponent boxing lessons, considerably honing the younger man's skills. The two men even fought exhibition contests in front of the other inmates and staff of the gaol. Choynski never won a title but his prison pupil went on to become one of the greatest of all heavyweight champions.

The Ghost Runner

In the 1950s, John Tarrant, who had been born in 1932, was an extremely promising long-distance runner in the north-east of England. He was also a keen amateur boxer. One summer he took part in a few fights at a travelling boxing booth, winning a total of £17 for lasting the distance against the booth fighters. All these bouts were completed before he was 20 years old. Before he went back to his amateur running, Tarrant contacted the Derbyshire Athletic Association, explained what he had done and asked to be reinstated as an amateur. He thought that this would be a formality but to his horror he was told by the national Amateur Athletic Association that because he had taken money for boxing he was now a professional athlete and could never compete at any sport as an amateur again.

Tarrant was horrified and did everything he could to be taken back into amateur running. The authorities were adamant. As far as long-distance running was concerned, Tarrant was now a pariah. However, the runner was a determined man and did his best to shame the officials of the sport into reinstating him. During the week he was working 12-hour shifts in a lime quarry as a labourer. On Saturdays he started turning up at long-distance road races all over the country, wearing a long overcoat and mingling with the crowd near the start line. Then as soon as a race had started, Tarrant would shed his coat, revealing that he was in athletics gear and join in the race, sprinting after the disappearing pack.

Soon John Tarrant became a fixture at all the major road races, spurned by the authorities but cheered on by the crowd. He was not allowed to break the tape at the finish but again and again Tarrant ended the race among the leaders, before turning off just before the finish line. Newspapers took up his cause. The *Daily Express* called him the 'Ghost Runner', and the name stuck.

In the end, after years of endeavour, the authorities yielded to public pressure. John Tarrant was allowed to compete as an amateur runner again. He celebrated by coming in second in the 1960 AAA Marathon. He looked forward eagerly to being selected as a member of the British Olympic squad. It was not to be. Tarrant's reinstatement applied only to Great Britain. As far as the international Olympic Association was concerned John Tarrant was still a professional.

Doggedly Tarrant went on running, competing in long-distance races in Great Britain, the USA and Africa. In 1970, he was the first white athlete to compete in and win the 50-mile race from Stanger to Durban in South Africa. He set world bests for the 40 and 100 miles distances.

However, John Tarrant's body had been broken as well as his heart. In 1975, he died of stomach cancer at the age of 42.

THE BIRDS

When Sugar Ray Leonard was matched against Ayub Kalule in Houston in June 1981, one of the bout's publicists tried to get newspaper space for the fight by producing someone he claimed to be a witch doctor who had placed a spell on Leonard. Disgusted by this, a boxing personality called Rock Newman held an open-air press conference to condemn the so-called spell. As he did so, he was attacked by a flock of angry crows, who forced him to flee.

'FAT AND HORIZONTAL'

When British heavyweight champion Don Cockell was described as a 'fat and horizontal lay-about' and also as 'overweight and flabby,' by a lead writer in the *Daily Mail* on

26 April 1956, the boxer took exception to the description and sued. He claimed that the remarks meant that he had no regard for the reputation of his country or of British boxing. The defendants held that the remarks were not defamatory but represented fair comment on their part.

The furore occurred as a result of Cockell's bout with a Tongan heavyweight, Kitione Lave, whose pre-boxing career had included mowing the lawns of Queen Salote on his home island. Cockell had previously lost to world heavyweight champion Rocky Marciano and leading contender Nino Valdez and was approaching the end of his time as a professional boxer. His bout with Lave was to be his last.

A doctor and a sparring partner gave evidence to the effect that Cockell had been fit when he had fought Lave but sports writers and experts, including former champion Len Harvey, gave it as their opinions that Cockell had been overweight and sluggish for the contest.

Summing up, the Lord Chief Justice told the jury that Cockell might have had difficulty in getting weight off during training, but the point was whether or not he had tried. His lordship pointed out that after initially being knocked down with a punch to the jaw Cockell had got up again six times.

After an absence of about half an hour, the jury found for the plaintiff. Don Cockell was awarded £7,500 and costs.

How Many Rounds?

In a bid for publicity, in 1938 middleweight Frank Hough announced that he would fight a 10-round contest every week. For a while he stuck to his itinerary, fighting regularly in London until 14 February. His next bout was scheduled for 17 February, three days later. The match was vetoed by the British Boxing Board of Control, which stipulated that there must be a seven-day gap between each 10-round contest. Hough and his manager circumnavigated this ban by announcing that the second fight would be over nine rounds instead. Hough defeated a French boxer, Marcel Bazin, on points.

HIGH DIVE

In 1924, an American middleweight called Jock Malone (1897–1964) was matched in Boston with the travelling Welsh boxer Frank Moody. Malone was so confident of victory that upon his arrival in the city he told sports writers that if he did not defeat the Welshman he would dive fully clothed from the bridge over the Charles River into the water below.

In the event Moody won the contest on points over 10 rounds. Malone left Boston hurriedly, without keeping his promise. However, in that same year he returned to the city to meet former champion Johnny Wilson. Cynical writers asked Malone if he would jump into the river this time if he lost. Again the middleweight promised to do so.

On 29 July, Wilson knocked out Malone in the sixth round. In his post-match interviews Malone would neither confirm nor deny that he would jump from the bridge into the river, he merely told the members of the press to meet him at the bridge the following morning. Bright and early, Malone met the assembled writers. He was wearing a smart summer outfit, complete with straw hat. Without a word, Jock Malone climbed on to the rail across the bridge and jumped, feet first, 63ft into the river below. Then he swam to the bank, scrambled out and climbed up to the bridge again. Once more he jumped into the water. Coming back up for the second time he told the writers that he was a man of his word. He had lost twice in Boston, so he had jumped into the city's river twice, as he had promised.

HELLGATE AND THE TINMAN

Bill Hooper from Bristol laboured in a tin works, so during his ring career he was known as the Fighting Tinman. He was sponsored by the notorious rake Lord Barrymore who was known as 'Hellgate'. Hooper combined his ring duties with acting as Barrymore's bodyguard. In this capacity he attended many of the orgies visited by his master and the Prince of Wales.

On one occasion Barrymore and Hooper went in search of a writer called Fox, who had lampooned the peer in a broadsheet. They found Fox with the Prince of Wales at Brighton. Barrymore and Fox started fighting. The Prince of Wales insisted that they have a proper prize fight. The prince seconded Barrymore and Hooper made sure that no one interfered. Fox began to look like he would win the fight, so Barrymore kicked him. This action disgusted the Prince of Wales and he abandoned the contest.

Hooper lost all credibility as a prizefighter in 1795, when he fought Big Ben Brain. After the first few rounds it was obvious that the Tinman was completely outclassed by his opponent. Lord Barrymore, who had wagered heavily on Hooper, called out 'Save the bets, Bill!' Accordingly, in order to prolong the contest, Hooper ran from his opponent, falling every time he was touched by Brain. In this way he lasted for over two hours, until darkness fell. The match was declared a draw. All bets were said to be null and void and Lord Barrymore saved a fortune.

Hooper's association with Barrymore and his coterie finished his career. Once he was persuaded by the aristocrats to attend a social occasion dressed as a clergyman and then disgust the other guests with a stream of oaths and profanity. He was arrested on a number of occasions while trying to cover up some of his master's notorious escapades.

Lord Barrymore died after a freak accident with a gun when he was only 24. Hooper could not find another patron and drifted into a life of drunken poverty. One night he was discovered unconscious in a London street. He came round long enough to try to say his name – 'Hoop... Hoop...' before being carried to a workhouse, where he died.

MEN OF THE CLOTH: 3 – GEORGE FOREMAN

George Foreman, known in his earlier days as 'Big Bad George', won an Olympic gold medal at heavyweight in Mexico City in 1968 and went on to hold the World Heavyweight Championship from 1973 and then lost it in dramatic circumstances to Muhammad Ali, making a comeback in 1974, in the celebrated Zaire 'Rumble in the Jungle'. In his early days Foreman deliberately cultivated a mean, sullen demeanour and was feared for his savage approach in the ring. He fought on after losing to Ali, although his confidence and self-esteem had both suffered considerably. In 1977 he underwent a religious conversion.

Foreman had lost a close and hard-fought decision in Puerto Rico to Jimmy Young. In his dressing room after the bout he felt physically and emotionally drained. He was suffering from cuts to his face and could hardly stand. Suddenly he felt as if he had died spiritually and needed some form of religious rebirth. He cried out 'Jesus is coming alive in me' and decided to devote the rest of his life to the service of the Lord.

He sold his house and cars and no longer travelled first-class in aircraft. At a mass meeting in Los Angeles he told a congregation of 3,000 of his intention. He had to send someone out to buy him a Bible, so that he could start studying the scriptures. Foreman started attending church services regularly. He married his long-time girlfriend and shaved off his beard and hair to signify his change of life. He became an evangelist and appeared on television and at meetings all over the USA. He was ordained a minister in the Church of the Lord Jesus Christ. He then sold a tractor for $25,000 and used the proceeds to buy a plot of dilapidated land upon which he built his first church. He also established a youth and community centre in Houston.

Foreman served his community for almost ten years and then, with his church in need of money, he made a boxing comeback. By this time his weight had ballooned and his personality had been transformed to that of a jovial, middle-aged man. Despite the scepticism of the press, he won 24 contests, 23 of them inside the distance. In 1991 he lost a challenge for the heavyweight title to champion Evander Holyfield. Three years later he regained his title, at 45 the oldest man to become heavyweight champion, by knocking out Michael Moorer in the 10th round. Before he could fight Moorer, Foreman had been forced to go to court to stop the controlling bodies from preventing him from boxing because of his age. In 1997, Foreman retired from boxing but made a fortune as the television salesman for a grilling machine.

So Sue Me!

Teddy Baldock, a popular East London bantamweight, was matched in 1930 at the Albert Hall against Emile Pladner, a professional sculptor who briefly had held a version of the world flyweight title. The bout was promoted by Jeff Dickson, an enterprising American who was busy in Europe at the time. For 6 rounds Baldock boxed on the defensive, letting Pladner do most of the work. In the 6th round Pladner knocked the English fighter down with a punch to the body. Baldock writhed on the canvas, complaining that he had been hit low. The referee disqualified Pladner.

Jeff Dickson was furious, accusing Baldock of acting. Baldock sued the promoter for libel and won the case. Dickson was forced to pay costs and to print a public apology. It turned out to be a pyrrhic victory. Dickson never employed Baldock as a fighter at the Albert Hall again.

'Are You Doing Anything Tomorrow?'

Tommy Farr became heavyweight champion of Great Britain and the British Empire and took world champion Joe Louis the full 15-round distance. In 1932, however, he was just another young light heavyweight on the Welsh professional boxing circuit. On 30 December he fought a spirited 15-round draw at Trealaw, Mid-Glamorgan, against Jerry Daley, a former middleweight champion of Wales. Farr was feeling pleased with himself after the bout but was soon brought down to earth when he was approached by the promoter. During their contest Daley had sustained a badly cut eye and would be out of action for a few weeks. The problem was that Daley had been so sure that he would defeat a young upstart like Farr that he had booked himself to fight again the next evening against Charlie Bundy, a leading Welsh light heavyweight.

The promoter told Farr that as he was responsible for Daley's injury it was now his responsibility to take the incapacitated boxer's place and fight Bundy himself. In vain, Tommy Farr protested. It was made plain to him that if he did not enter the ring against Bundy the next evening, the Welsh promoters, upon whom he depended for his livelihood, would be reluctant to give him any more fights.

Reluctantly Farr agreed. The following night he defeated Charlie Bundy on points over 15 rounds at Treherbert. It was his second 15-round bout on consecutive evenings while he was still a teenager.

LADIES FIRST

Before she became Britain's first licensed professional woman boxer, Jane Couch 'the Fleetwood Assassin' worked in a Blackpool rock factory. She fought in the USA and on the mainland of Europe and then applied to the British Boxing Board of Control for a licence to box in Great Britain. The Board turned down her application on medical grounds, stating that pre-menstrual tension made women unstable. Jane Couch took the Board to an industrial tribunal on grounds of sexual discrimination. In 1998 she won her case and was granted a licence.

THE ANTI-BOXING LOBBY

'Boxing might have been going on in New York right now if the men who had charge of the clubs had handled it with credit. They made the mistake by not stopping contests when they became brutal, or when it was manifest to all that one of the contestants had no possible chance of winning.'

Theodore Roosevelt, then Vice President of the USA, in 1901.

'A large number of disreputable characters, especially bad women from the underworld, flocked to the city. More than 60 women were arrested and imprisoned after the fight to protect the health and morals of the city. Leading hotels and cafés openly violated the state prohibition law. In all parts of the city, where boys congregated, fights occurred of an angry nature.'

A Toledo clergyman after the Jess Willard–Jack Dempsey title fight in the city in 1919.

'WHY AREN'T YOU IN THE TRENCHES?'

Tom Cowler was a very promising young British heavyweight from Cumbria. He strung together so many victories over other heavyweights that he decided to try his luck in the USA. Unfortunately, the year that he chose for his departure was 1914, the date of the outbreak of the First World War. Many thought that he had fled to avoid service in the armed forces. This accusation ruined the young man's career.

Matters came to a head when Cowler was matched against a leading American, Gunboat Smith, a former seaman in the US Pacific Fleet. Before their fight could even start, Smith's manager Jim Buckley started shouting loudly, 'Fight him hard, Gunboat! Remember, you were there when your country wanted you, right on Uncle Sam's battleship. You didn't run away at the first sign of danger.'

The partisan crowd began jeering at the Englishman. Cowler could not concentrate on his boxing and was well beaten over ten rounds. The *Des Moines Register* commented, 'There is no doubt that Buckley's verbal attack caused Cowler's mind to wander, for he is tired of being asked why he isn't in the trenches.'

Cowler fought on, but he had lost the sympathy of the crowds and he was never the same fighter again. He remained in the USA for the remainder of the war. He retired from boxing in 1925 and died in 1951, at the age of 59.

TRAIN OF EVENTS

In November 1873, Tom Allen, who claimed the American bare-knuckle heavyweight championship, was matched against Ben Hogan. Boxing was illegal in the USA but subsequent events proved how popular the sport was and the length to which fight fans would go to witness bouts.

It was decided that the bout would be held in St Joseph, Missouri, where promoters assured the protagonists that not only would there be 'a fair field and no favour' for the fighters but that local law-enforcement officers could be persuaded to turn a blind eye to activities outside the town. A special train was chartered to carry Allen and Hogan and their backers and seconds and also a vast crowd of would-be spectators.

When the train reached its destination it was met by an assembly of public-spirited citizens and militia declaring that there would be no fight. The Governor of Missouri himself forbade the contest.

Undeterred, the occupants of the train promptly hired a steamboat and set off up-river to find a spot where the fight could take place. The authorities in Kansas and Nebraska ordered the captain to continue on his voyage. Troops from an army barracks were lined up on the shore to emphasise the rebuttal.

As a last resort the backers of the fight decided to try to hold it in Iowa. The boat headed for the town of Council Bluffs. On the morning of 18 November, the Governor of Iowa received a panic-stricken telegram from a number of citizens of Council Bluffs. It said, 'The Allen–Hogan prize fight is to take place on Tuesday in Iowa and the men are here. We are powerless to prevent it.' It was further reported that over 1,500 toughs from the east had arrived to witness the bout and that they were terrorising the town.

When the fight entourage arrived at Council Bluffs, they boarded another train. The local sheriff and a handful of deputies were deployed to stop it and arrest everyone on board. The passengers merely laughed at the officers of the law and ordered the engineer to take the train a few miles up the track, where the fight could take place. Bravely the sheriff insisted on travelling on the train to keep order. The conductor refused to take him unless he bought a ticket. Neither the lawman nor his assistants had any money, so the train pulled out of Council Bluffs unimpeded.

Finally, the train stopped at the small town of Pacific City, 16 miles down the line. A ring was set up. Shortly before the bout was due to start, the sheriff of Mills County arrived with some deputies and ordered the crowd to disperse. The lawmen were roughly handled and the contest got under way. After three violent rounds Hogan claimed that he had been fouled by his opponent. The crowd started fighting. Knives and pistols were drawn. It was decided to call the decision a draw.

One-Round Wonders

Fight fans prefer their bouts to go a few rounds in order to get value for money, but occasionally bouts lasting only one round have been entertaining or bizarre enough for most spectators.

Jack Dempsey v. Fireman Jim Flynn, 13 February 1917, Salt Lake City, Utah

In 1917, hard-punching Jack Dempsey was an up-and-coming heavyweight, who was to win the world championship several years later. In Salt Lake City he met a veteran fighter called Fireman Jim Flynn, who had lost to Tommy Burns and Jack Johnson, both world champions in their day. Several days before the fight, Dempsey was working in a bowling alley when someone dropped a heavy ball on to his hand, smashing several fingers.

In need of the money, Dempsey went ahead with the contest, which was to be the main event on the bill. After the preliminary contests were over there was a 45-minute delay before Flynn and Dempsey entered the ring. There were rumours that the two principals and their backers had been arguing about money in the box office.

As soon as the bout started, Flynn waded in and knocked Dempsey down with a right cross. Flynn stood over the fallen man and when Dempsey staggered to his feet, he knocked him down again. Altogether Flynn knocked Dempsey down six times before Dempsey's brother, who was acting as his second, threw in the towel to signify Dempsey's retirement.

It was a shock result, as Flynn was regarded as being over the hill. Dempsey blamed his loss on his injured hand and the fact that his brother had thrown in the towel too soon. Jack Dempsey's wife Maxine had a different story to tell. In several Utah saloons over the next few nights she told anyone willing to buy her a drink that her husband had accepted $500 to take a dive in order to pay off his debts.

Dempsey never fought in Utah again, but a year later he knocked Flynn out in the first round in a return contest. He was never knocked out again in his career.

Muhammad Ali v. Sonny Liston, 25 May 1965,
Lewiston, Maine
After Muhammad Ali had unexpectedly taken the heavyweight title from Sonny Liston in February 1964, it was more than a year before he defended it for the first time, against him. In the interim, he had got married, travelled to Africa and suffered a double hernia in training. Many venues refused to host the match because of Ali's conversion to the Muslim faith and because his first win over Liston was largely regarded as a fluke. In the end, the bout took place over a high school ice hockey rink in Lewiston, Maine.

Ali's title defence lasted for two minutes. After some desultory sparring, the challenger flopped to the canvas. Most of the spectators had not seen the punch that floored Liston. There were cries of 'Fake!' from the crowd. Liston got up after the timekeeper had counted to 10, but the referee, former champion Jersey Joe Walcott, had not picked up the official's count properly and allowed the bout to continue. Nat Fleischer, the influential editor of *Ring* magazine, hammered on the canvas and, with completely no authority, ordered Walcott to declare a knockout. The referee did so and Ali was adjudged to have retained his crown.

The right-hand blow with which Ali had brought the match to an end was called 'the Phantom Punch'. Many declared that it had never landed, and that if it had it was not powerful enough to floor such a strong man as Liston. Others held that it had been the perfect punch, thrown so quickly that most spectators – and Liston – never saw it coming.

A Challenge

Sam Langford, a black Canadian fighter was reckoned by many to have been the greatest fighter never to have won the world heavyweight championship. In 1913 he was touring Australia, challenging all the local heavyweights. At Rockhampton in Queensland in June he boxed a draw with Colin Bell, an up-and-coming Australian heavyweight. Langford thought that he had won and challenged Bell to a 75-yard sprint race to decide who was the better man. In front of the same crowd that had watched them fight, the two men raced. The result was adjudged a tie.

Another Challenge

Tom Cribb was one of the greatest of all bare-knuckle champions but he had not fought for a long time. Most people thought that he had retired to devote his time to his successful London tavern. Taking advantage of this belief a younger fighter, Bill Neat, claimed the championship of England.

This infuriated Cribb. One day after a well-attended benefit boxing tournament, Cribb leapt into the ring clutching a bundle of banknotes. The champion was portly and out of condition but still considered himself the best fighter in the land. 'Gentlemen!' he thundered, 'I have only just learned that William Neat has claimed the championship, which he says I'm too old and fat to hold any longer. Gentlemen, my blood boils at this insult and I've come here tonight at the earliest possible moment after hearing of this insolent claim to say that as long as I've a drop of blood in my veins and a breath in my body, I'll yield the championship to no man living without a fight. If Neat wants to call himself Champion he'll have to beat me first; and here's my money, ready to any amount!'

Fortunately calmer heads prevailed. Tom Cribb was persuaded to retire. Even so, he had the last laugh. He nominated his protégé Tom Spring as his successor, not Bill Neat.

DESPAIRING REMARKS FROM THE MC

'Welcome to lovely downtown Warrington!'
'Gentlemen are asked to moderate their language!'
'Let's have a big hand for a gallant loser!'
'Kindly keep your seats!'
'Could we please have the missing charity collection box back?'
'Entertainment during the interval will be provided by Karloff the Cossack and his piano-accordian.'

Projectile Vomiting?

Cruiserweight Chris Jackson lost his gum-shield and had to use a replacement in a bout at Burton upon Trent in 2006. It did not fit properly and he spat it out five times in a single round. The referee disqualified him.

Excessive Brutality

Light heavyweights 'Prince' Charles Williams and his opponent Merqui Sosa put up a titanic struggle in their Atlantic City bout in January 1995. By the 7th round both men were reeling helplessly around the ring, too weary to exchange further punches. The doctor at ringside, Frank Doggett, decided that the fighters had imposed excessive punishment on each other and that neither was in any state to continue. He ordered the referee to stop the fight. The official did so and declared a verdict of a technical draw.

Please Release Me!

Most of the twentieth-century boxers who tried to get away from their managers usually found that they were bound to their handlers with hoops of steel. Soon after the First World War, however, the British heavyweight champion Joe Beckett made a determined effort to secure his freedom from his manager Bernard Mortimer.

An action took place in the Chancery Division of the High Court in which Mortimer tried to prevent Beckett from handling his own affairs independently. Mortimer declared that Beckett had signed a contract with him in 1914 in which, in exchange for a token sum of ten shillings he gave the manager full rights for seven years to handle all the fighter's boxing matters. Beckett promised that he would pay Mortimer 50 per cent of all purses above £25 and 50 per cent of all music hall fees received. Beckett acknowledged in the contract that he had received monetary assistance from Mortimer over the last five years which they had been together. Five years later, in 1919, Beckett had written to Mortimer seeking to break this contract. The letter was produced in court:

> Dear Mortimer, I have decided that for the future I shall manage my own business, as I find that our present business relationship has a tendency to prevent me from putting my best efforts into my work. . . .

Mortimer had refused to sever the relationship. He told the court that for some years after 1911 Beckett had seldom earned more than £10 or £15 for a contest. In 1919, however, he had received £2,500 for a bout with Frank Goddard. Now that Beckett was earning good money, Mortimer felt entitled to half of all the fighter's earnings.

When questioned, Beckett admitted that he could not read until he had joined the army during the war and could only write his name because Mortimer had shown him how to do so in order to sign contracts put before him. He claimed that Mortimer had read to him some contracts which he had signed but that he had discovered afterwards that the contents of the documents had not been as Mortimer had claimed. He would not have bound himself for seven years as Mortimer had claimed.

Beckett's barrister said that the contract was an extraordinary document. It did not bind Mortimer to anything, yet for seven years Beckett had to do everything that the manager told him to. Beckett had tied himself hand and foot for seven years as far as boxing was concerned.

Giving judgement Mr Justice Russell agreed. There was no mutuality in the contract. It was difficult to specify anything that the contract made Mortimer do. The manager's motion was dismissed and Joe Beckett was freed from his contractual bonds.

THE NUMBERS GAME

In the 1930s there were over 3,000 registered professional boxers in Great Britain. In 2009 there were 742.

WHEN PUSH COMES TO SHOVE

Going into the 12th round of their North American Boxing Federation world light middleweight championship bout, champion Julio César Green of the Dominican Republic and challenger Lonnie Beasley were in close contention. They were also exhausted. Both men went into a clinch. Referee Vic Drakulich stepped between them and pushed the boxers apart. It was all too much for Beasley. The light middleweight staggered back and fell to the floor. He remained there, too tired to get up. The referee hesitated for a moment and then counted Beasley out, awarding the fight to Green. One of Beasley's seconds was so infuriated that he chased Drakulich out of the ring. Nevertheless, the verdict stood, which was more than Beasley could do.

UNITED

Between the two world wars, there were several unsuccessful attempts to form a boxers' union. The National Union of Boxers had former world flyweight champion Jimmy Wilde as its president and British middleweight, light heavyweight and heavyweight champion Len Harvey as its vice-president. Before its demise it issued a list of its achievements:

Enforced the N.U.B. minimums of £1 for six; £1/10s/0d for eight; and £2/10s/0d for ten rounds in many halls where they were not paid before.

Secured agreements from the National Sporting Club, Wembley Stadium, Harringay, and many other promotions that 'seconds' money' will not be demanded from boxers. (This alone is worth much more to boxers than the 1/- a month Union subscription).

Provided members with insurance against ring and other accidents, and sickness, for the first time in the history of the sport.

Provided members with dependable managers.

Provided many members with contests.

Won many claims for members in court and before the Board of Control.

Prevented the taking of unfair commissions from boxers' purses.

Secured the support of leading newspaper sports writers for the boxers' demands for fair play and justice.

Secured the active support of a growing number of Members of Parliament and influential sportsmen for the boxers' demands.

Four champions – Tommy Farr, Jake Kilrain, Jimmy Walsh and Johnny McGory belong to the N.U.B. So do many other top-liners. If these 'stars' find the Union useful to them, so will you.

WHO'S WINNING?

When NBC televised the world heavyweight championship bout between Muhammad Ali and Earnie Shavers at Madison Square Garden in 1977, they adopted a new method of scoring by actually flashing the judges' scores on to the screen at the end of each round. Ali's backers stationed a man in front of a television set in the dressing room. He kept relaying the scores to Ali's corner men, who were able to plan the champion's schedule accordingly, so that he won on points. 'Why didn't we think of that?' asked Shavers after the fight. 'Guess Ali never missed a trick.'

THE COMMON INFORMER

The position of common informer went back to the time of Edward III (1312–77). In order to restrain merchants from selling their wares after a fair was officially over, officials declared that anyone who sued such a merchant successfully could claim part of his fine. As time went on, more powers were added to the list. By the 1930s one of the most lucrative fields for common informers was that of the Sunday Observance Act. Promoters of entertainments on Sunday could be sued.

A leading, financially successful common informer was a clerk called Alfred William Green, who changed his name to Anthony Houghton le Touzel. He admitted that he did not care what people did on Sundays. His lawsuits were for personal gain. Over the course of a few years he brought more than 200 successful actions against showmen and promoters. In 1935, he turned his attention to stopping professional boxing shows on Sunday afternoons, and in the process further enriching himself.

The object of his intentions was the Ring boxing stadium in Blackfriars. Sunday shows had been a feature of London entertainment for years. The promoter was a woman, Bella Burge, who had carried on with the running of boxing after the death of her husband Dick, during the First World War. Green conducted his own case and sued a number of officials at the Ring for working on Sundays. Those attacked in this way were the matchmaker and announcer and the printer of programmes. Before the case could get under way, Bella Burge announced that if Green should be successful she would pay all the fines involved.

Boxing was very popular in the East End of London and there were rumours that Green, the common informer, was about to be menaced by members of the underworld, who were also fight fans. The police placed Green under their protection and he won the case. The people named in the case were duly fined and Sunday boxing was banned at the Ring.

Looking for a Fight

Second Lieutenant Belas, stationed with the First Battalion of the East Yorkshire Regiment in India, was a keen amateur boxer. In 1936, he decided to enter the Indian Army championships in the featherweight class. The problem was that the tournament was being held in Bombay, while Second Lieutenant Belas was soldiering in Waziristan, 1,500 miles away. This did not deter the young officer. He crossed the rough and often dangerous terrain in a number of ways – by train, on foot, in lorries. After some weeks he reached Bombay, only to find that he was the only entrant in the featherweight division and had no opponents. Belas entered the next weight class up – the lightweight – and won it. Then he set out on the journey back to his barracks.

Damn Yankees!

'The American ring is a business pure and simple; the fighting is a business, not an art; the amount of betting associated with it is degrading and nullifies all true sport; while the boxer who can conceive a new method of stopping his opponent, whether semi-fair or foul, is glorified if it goes with the money on the ringside.'

Letter to The Times, *17 January 1911.*

'Smeared with a Substance'

Veteran welterweight Shane Mosley was about to fight Mexican Antonio Margarito for the WBA welterweight championship in Los Angeles in January 2009, before a crowd of 20,000. His corner men routinely examined Margarito's hand bandages. What they saw caused them to complain bitterly to the officials in charge of the bout. The Mexican was made to change his bandages, while the original wrappings were confiscated. Mosley went on to score an unexpected 9th-round stoppage.

A month later the California State Athletic Association revoked Margarito's licence for a year and that of his trainer for putting plaster-like substances on the Mexican's gloves, which would have hardened as the match progressed and almost literally would have given Margarito 'hands of stone'.

State inspectors in charge of the match said that they had taken two gauze pads from Margarito's hands that were 'smeared with a substance.' They had been inserted under the knuckle portion of the hand bandages. Margarito denied all knowledge of the matter, saying that all he had done had been to hold up his fists for his trainer to bandage before the fight. The State Commission disagreed. 'When you're the top dog, you bear some responsibility for your team,' they told the suspended boxer.

CHESS BOXING

It started as a far-fetched storyline in a comic strip and then was translated into reality in different countries. In 2008, the UK Chessboxing Club was opened in Islington, London. Members box for two minutes and then play chess for four minutes, alternating until 11 rounds have gone by or one of the players has been knocked out or checkmated.

BOXING BILLINGS

The Rumble in the Jungle: Muhammad Ali v. George Foreman, Zaire, 30 October 1974

The Thriller in Manila: Muhammad Ali v. Joe Frazier, Philippines, 1 October 1975

The World Awaits: Oscar de la Hoya v. Floyd Mayweather Jnr, Las Vegas, 5 May 2007

Path to Glory: Miguel Angel Huerta v. Mario Angel Perez, Coron, California, 17 September 2004

The Saint Valentine's Day Massacre: Sugar Ray Robinson v. Jake LaMotta, Chicago Stadium, Chicago, Illinois, 14 February 1951

KNUCKLES, NOT GLOVES

Twenty-four-year-old Tongan heavyweight Kitione Lave's boxing career was going through a quiet phase when he signed up to take part in a bare-knuckle fight against Hugh Burton at Doncaster Greyhound Stadium. As soon as the bout was advertised, both men were arrested and bound over by the magistrates for conduct likely to cause a breach of the peace. The chief prosecuting solicitor pointed out, 'It is a criminal offence to take part in a prize fight in this country and renders the guilty person liable to considerable terms of imprisonment.'

The two men had agreed to fight for £500 a side. When asked how many rounds he had intended to fight, Lave answered, '15 or a hundred. I don't mind.' Burton replied, 'A fight to the finish.'

SHOULDN'T YOU BE AT SCHOOL?

A boxing phenomenon of the 1920s and '30s was 'Nipper' Pat Daly, who had his first professional bout at the age of 9. His career was virtually over by the time he was 17. Spotted by a tough old-school trainer, 'Professor' Andrew Newton, Daly fought in London halls by night and attended school in the daytime. By the age of 14 he had left school and was fighting once a fortnight full-time. Starting as an 8 stone flyweight, Daly soon went up to featherweight. He won so many fights that he was offered a world title shot in the USA, but Newton felt that his protégé was not quite ready.

At the age of 16, Daly met the British champion Johnny Cuthbert in a non-title fight. He experienced difficulty making the weight but was ahead for the first eight rounds before Cuthbert caught up with the youth and knocked him out. A number of fight followers, including former world champion Jimmy Wilde, felt that Daly was being brought along too quickly, but his trainer Newton would have none of it. Then Daly was matched with a future British featherweight champion, Seaman Tommy Watson, but lost when the towel was thrown in from his corner in the 13th round.

Daly was concussed during the fight. For a time he lost the use of his legs but made a recovery. At once Newton matched him against a Welsh boxer called Nobby Baker. Still concussed from the Watson fight, Daly was stopped in the 13th round.

Disillusioned, Daly broke away from Newton and fought on under a new manager, but the spark seemed to have gone. He had taken too many beatings too early in his career. He retired from boxing at the age of 17 and opened a gymnasium. Over the course of his fighting career he had taken part in 120 contests, won 100, lost 11 and drawn 8.

THE WINNER

In November 2008, Peter Buckley outpointed Matin Mohammed at Birmingham. It was a milestone in Buckley's career. It was Buckley's 300th contest, of which he had lost 256 – 88 of them in successive bouts.

WHAT'S IN A NAME?

By the beginning of 2009 a new British heavyweight had appeared on the scene. He was 6ft 8in tall, weighed 18 stone and had won his first two professional contests inside the distance. The jury was still out as to how good he was going to be, but everyone agreed that he had the ideal name for a boxer – Tyson Fury.

UNDEFEATED

A few world champions have retired undefeated throughout their careers, including World Heavyweight Champion Rocky Marciano, lightweight champion Jack McAuliffe, paperweight champion Jim Barry and light welterweight champion Terry Marsh.

In 2009, Welshman Joe Calzaghe retired as unbeaten WBO super middleweight champion of the world at the age of 36. Throughout his professional career he had had 46 bouts, winning them all. He won the title from Chris Eubank in 1997 and went on to win 23 consecutive world title fights. Throughout his professional career he had been trained by his father.

TIME TO SAY GOODBYE

Henry Maske was one of the most popular of all German boxers. He won a middleweight gold medal at the 1988 Seoul Olympics. After he had turned professional he won the IBF version of the world light heavyweight championship and defended it 11 times. In 1996, he announced that he was going to defend his title for the last time. The bout took place at the Olympiahalle in Munich, Germany. Maske lost on a split decision. The evening, however, was not a total loss. Before the bout started, Sarah Brightman and Andrea Bocelli sang the song 'Time To Say Goodbye' to Maske from the ring. Their version of the song was an enormous success with the crowd and the vast television audience. The record went on to sell almost three million copies in Germany and made a star of the hitherto almost unknown Bocelli.

THE BEAST FROM THE EAST

The boxing public has always liked its heavyweights to be big. Some have been enormous but few of the giants turned out to be successful boxers. In the 1950s, South African Ewart Poltgeiter, 7ft 2in tall and weighing 330lb, was introduced to England as a heavyweight prospect by promoter Jack Solomons. Poltgeiter flattered only to deceive. He won a few contests but, not unnaturally, proved to be slow and ponderous. He won a few fights but did not enthuse the crowds. Poltgeiter retired with a record of 11 wins 2 losses and a draw.

Until the twenty-first century, the biggest heavyweight champion was the Italian Primo Carnera, who stood 6ft 6in tall and weighed 270lb. He was mob-connected and there were rumours that many of his fights were 'fixed'.

The latest big man to attract interest has been a Russian, Nikolai Valuev. When he won the World Boxing Association version of the world heavyweight championship in 2005, he was the tallest and heaviest man ever to win the title. Scaling 7ft in height, at a weight of 23 stone, Valuev towered over his opponent, the American John Ruiz, as he won on points. With his huge jaw, shaven head and tough features he presented an awesome figure in the ring.

He was born in Leningrad, later St Petersburg, in 1973, the son of a factory worker. By the time he was 12 years old he was already well over 6ft tall, although he was still very thin. At first Valuev concentrated on basketball, but then started putting on weight and decided to turn to the more lucrative sport of boxing at the relatively advanced age of 20. He had a few amateur contests and then in 2003 was signed up by the influential German promoter Wilfried Sauerland.

At first, because of his grotesque size, Valuev was regarded as more of a circus performer than a genuine professional boxer. However, he became an enormous attraction among boxing fans and fought at venues all over the world, including Germany, Russia, the USA, Japan, Korea, Australia and Czechoslovakia. At the same time he was being carefully matched by his promoter and started to beat a number of leading European and American heavyweights. By the time he challenged John Ruiz for the title, Nikolai Valuev had knocked out 23 of his opponents and beaten the rest on points.

He settled in the USA and was taken up by the wily American promoter Don King, causing one sports writer to remark, 'King has found his Kong!' In 2007, Valuev suffered his first defeat, losing his championship to another Russian, Ruslan Chagaev, on points. However, Valuev was soon back on the winning trail. In 2008 he won the WBA heavyweight title back again. Chagaev had been forced to relinquish the title through injury. Valuev outpointed another former world champion, Evander Holyfield, to make his boxing record 50 wins and 1 loss, with 35 victories inside the distance.

Weight Problems

Ricky Hatton, 'the Hitman', was one of the most popular and charismatic boxers of the early years of the twenty-first century, winning over 40 contests. From his base in Manchester he won different versions of the world light welterweight and welterweight titles. Throughout his career, however, he suffered from weight problems. Between bouts he would put on as much as 40lb. Much of this was due to Hatton's passion for fried food and Guinness.

Happy Talk

Amir Khan became one of Britain's best prospects after he won a silver medal at the 2004 Athens Olympics in the lightweight class. He was only 17 years old. He turned professional and ran up a series of inside-the-distance victories. In 2008 he suffered a setback when he was knocked out in the first round by Breidis Prescott, a fighter from Colombia. He then came back and won several more contests. Even when things were going badly for him, Khan had one consolation. In a poll conducted by the *Independent* newspaper he had come 22nd in a list of Britain's happiest people!

Pac-Man

Filipino boxer Manny Pacquiao is rated as one of the world's outstanding boxers. He won world titles at four different weights – flyweight, super bantamweight, super featherweight and lightweight. He fought his way out of poverty to such an extent that when he knocked out Britain's Ricky Hatton in 2009, he was guaranteed £10 million for his night's work, excluding his cut of the pay-per-view television receipts. In 2007 he ran for congress in his own country, funding his campaign with his own money. He received 75,908 votes to his opponent's 139,061 votes.

BARE-KNUCKLE CHAMPIONS

For over 150 years before the development of modern gloved boxing, bare-knuckle fighting was a very popular, if illegal, sport in Britain. A round ended when a contestant was floored, or fell down, and bouts could last hundreds of rounds in this fashion. Records from this era are sketchy and sometimes contradictory, but the champions of these primitive days are generally held to have been:

1719–30, James Figg

Sponsored by the Earl of Peterborough, Figg opened several schools of arms in London, where he taught and gave exhibitions of fencing, single-stick combat and bare-knuckle fighting. He challenged anyone at these sports for 'love, money or a bellyful.' His business card was designed by the artist William Hogarth. He defeated Ned Sutton three times to gain recognition as first champion of England. He died in 1734.

1730–5, Tom Pipes

Boxing was still an obscure sport after the retirement of Figg and little interest was shown when Pipes claimed the championship, the first of many to do so over the succeeding years. He twice defeated George Gretting, who also claimed the title.

1735–8, George Taylor

Another fighter of whom little is known, he opened a boxing booth in the Tottenham Court Road and claimed the title after the retirement of Figg. He was beaten in 20 minutes by Jack Broughton. Taylor died from internal injuries suffered in this bout.

1738–50, Jack Broughton

A protégé of James Figg, Broughton came to London from Gloucestershire. He drew up a set of rules for prize fighting and developed a form of 10oz boxing gloves, known as 'mufflers'. He became known as 'the Father of English Boxing'. After 12 years at the top he lost his title to Jack Slack and cost his patron the Duke of Cumberland £10,000 in lost bets, incurring the undying enmity of the king's son. He ended his years as one of the Yeomen of the Guard.

1750–60, Jack Slack

A crude, savage fighter specialising in a chopping blow to the napes of his opponents' necks, he held the title for ten years and engaged in the first international contest, defeating a Frenchman called Petit. Petit started strangling Slack but the champion escaped by kicking his opponent in the groin and later chasing him in triumph from the ring after 25 minutes. He lost the title to Bill Stevens. He ran a butcher's shop and died in 1768.

1760–1, William Stevens

A Birmingham fighter known as 'the Nailer', soon lost his title to George Meggs. Meggs had been coached by Jack Slack, who had lost his championship to Stevens. Slack admitted that he had bribed Stevens to surrender his title to Meggs. The disgraced Stevens had a few more bouts. He died in either 1781 or 1794.

1761–2, George Meggs

Notorious as a participant in England's first 'fixed' championship fight, Meggs lost twice to George Millsom and forfeited his title.

1762–5, George Millsom
Holding on to the title for three years, Millsom lost it to Tom Juchau after a 70-minute bout at St Albans.

1765–6, Tom Juchau
Defending his title nine months after he had won it, Juchau, whose day job was as a pavement-maker, was defeated in 40 minutes by Bill Darts at Guildford. The winning blow delivered by Darts was generally held to have been below the belt.

1766–9 and 1769–71 William Darts
In his first defence, Darts was defeated by Tom Lyons in 40 minutes. However, Lyons retired from the ring and Darts held on to his title for three years. He lost it in the first round to an Irishman, Peter Corcoran, although it was alleged that the champion had been bribed £100 to lose. He died in poverty in 1781.

1769, Tom Lyons
Does not seem to have fought again after his victory over Darts, preferring to return to his job on the River Thames as a waterman.

1771–6, Peter Corcoran
The Galway-born Corcoran lost his title after 38 rounds to Harry Sellars at Staines in Middlesex. He ran several pubs in London but things went badly for him and he was out of work when he died in 1784.

1776–9, Harry Sellers
Successfully defended his championship against Joe Hood and Bill Stevens before losing it in a little over a minute to Duggan Fearns, in what was probably yet another pre-arranged result.

1779–81, Duggan Fearns

A seafarer, Fearns presumably shared the low opinion of most of the spectators after his defeat of Sellars, because he went straight back to sea. There is no record of his ever having fought professionally again.

1783–91, Tom Johnson

Restoring credibility to the prize ring as an honest fighter, he won the vacant championship in 1783 in 15 minutes, defeating Jack Jarvis. Originally from Derby, he worked in London as a porter on the docks. Johnson defended the title on a number of occasions but started drinking and gambling, neglecting his training. He lost the championship to Big Ben Brain in 18 rounds. Afterwards he taught boxing in Ireland. Johnson died in 1797.

1791–4, Benjamin Brain

One of the first of the celebrated Bristol fighters, Big Ben Brain weighed 14 stone. The only person said to frighten him was his mother, a female blacksmith. He came to London and worked as a coal porter on the Thames wharf while building up a reputation as a fighter. He did not benefit from winning his championship, dying three years later, in 1794, of liver problems, without having defended it.

1794–5, Daniel Mendoza

Known variously as 'Mendoza the Jew' and 'the Light of Israel', Mendoza was the most skilful fighter of his generation and even wrote a treatise on the art of boxing. The Aldgate fighter claimed the title after defeating Bill Warr in 17 minutes. In the following year he lost the championship to John Jackson in 9 rounds at Hornchurch. He was one of the most popular of champions. He travelled with his own booth for much of his life, performed in a circus, worked as an army recruiting officer and was landlord of an inn. He had his last fight at the age of 52 and died in 1836.

1795, John Jackson

'Gentleman' John Jackson had only three fights but he brought much respectability to the sport, opening his own academy in Bond Street, where he taught many famous aristocrats, including Lord Byron, the Duke of Cumberland and Lord Chesterfield. He retired from the ring to concentrate on his academy and refereeing bouts. He died in 1845.

1796–7, Thomas Owen

Hopefully, Owen, a publican, claimed the title after Jackson's retirement, on the strength of a few minor victories. As soon as he met a more experienced and skilful fighter in Jack Bartholomew he lost any hold he might have had on the championship. He remained in the sport as a contestant and then as a notoriously harsh and brutal second. He died in 1843.

1797–1800, Jack Bartholomew

This fighter probably turned to the ring in search of a quiet life. He had stumbled into the role of bodyguard to the eccentric and homicidal Lord Camelford, who once had set out on a personal mission to assassinate Napoleon Bonaparte. Batholemew lost his title to the young and extremely promising Jem Belcher on Finchley Common. Later he displayed signs of what later would be called punch-drunkenness. He died in a poorhouse in 1803.

1800–3, Jem Belcher

One of the celebrated 'Bristol Boys' and a grandson of former champion Jack Slack, Belcher defended his title against Andrew Gamble, winning in five rounds on Wimbledon Common in 1800. He continued to win contests but, unfortunately, Belcher was blinded in one eye while playing rackets. He was forced to retire from the ring, but made a comeback against Hen Pearce, losing in 18 rounds. He died in 1811.

1804–6, Hen Pearce

Known as 'the Game Chicken' for his courage in the ring, the Bristolian claimed the title after defeating Joe Berks in 15 rounds. He defended his title successfully on a number of occasions but had a turbulent married life and took to drink. He retired, travelled with a booth and died at the age of 32 in 1809.

1807–8, John Gully

Bristol-born Gully, a butcher, was thrown into a debtors' prison where he achieved a reputation for fighting with his fists. The champion, Hen Pearce, bought Gully out of prison on condition that the latter fight him for the championship. Gully was beaten in 64 rounds but was generally regarded as the champion after Pearce's retirement. Gully had two more successful bouts and then retired to become successively a publican, landowner and Member of Parliament. He died in 1863 at the age of 79.

1809–22, Tom Cribb

After a spell in the navy and developing a ring reputation with a number of victories, Cribb claimed the title upon the retirement of Gully. He defended the championship on a number of occasions and achieved great fame after two controversial victories over Tom Molineaux, a former slave. He retired to become a successful London publican, where he was often attacked by patrons wishing to boast that they had hit Tom Cribb. He died in 1848.

1823–4, Tom Spring

Nominated for the championship by his mentor Tom Cribb, Spring lost a bout to Ned Painter, but Painter had been so badly damaged in the process that he would not fight Spring again, thus forfeiting his claim to the title. Spring, a methodical, cool-headed fighter, retired, never having been beaten again, in 1824. He became a successful landlord and died in 1851.

1824–5, Tom Cannon

The 'Great Gun of Windsor' claimed the title after the retirement of both Spring and Painter. In the following year he lost an epic fight with Jem Ward at Stony Stratford. He then cashed in on his fame as an actor in touring plays. Failing as a publican he took a job looking after swans. He died in 1858.

1825–7, Jem Ward

The 'Black Diamond' soon lost his championship to Peter Crawley, but the latter retired from the ring, so Ward continued to claim the title. He defended his championship successfully twice, toured the USA and then gave up prize fighting.

1827, Peter Crawley

It was not until he had been fighting for a decade that Crawley won the championship from Ward. He was known as 'the Young Rump Steak' because he was a butcher by trade. Deciding that he was putting too much of a strain on his body, Crawley abandoned the ring for his favourite pursuit of cock fighting. He bought a pub with money from his ring earnings, refereed fights and died in 1865.

1828–32, Jem Ward

Ward claimed the championship again and continued in business. He died at the age of 83 in 1884.

1833–9, James Burke

The 'Deaf 'Un' was a hearing-impaired, irresponsible, colourful character with a devastating punch. He claimed the title after knocking out the Irishman Simon Ward near St Albans in 1833. Ward later died from injuries sustained in the bout but Burke managed to escape a charge of causing his death. He lost his title to William Thompson. He died, poverty-stricken, in 1845.

1839–40, William Thompson

'Bendigo', so-called because he was one of triplets, the other two being nicknamed 'Shadrach' and 'Meshach', was a Nottingham fighter who defeated James Burke in 24 minutes in Leicestershire and thus became champion. He was backed by a fearsome gang of thugs known as 'the Nottingham Lambs', who did their best to intimidate their man's opponents. Bendigo then retired briefly and Burke reclaimed the title.

1840–1, Ben Caunt

One of the biggest of the early champions, he had three vicious contests with Bendigo, each one ending on a foul. When Bendigo announced his retirement, Caunt claimed the title but wasn't widely recognised as champion.

1841, Nick Ward

A younger brother of former champion Jem Ward, Nick Ward won the title on a foul against Deaf Burke when the crowd invaded the ring to save him from further punishment. His lucky streak continued when Ward defended his dubiously won title against Ben Caunt and won on a foul, but Caunt gained his revenge in a return bout, stopping the champion in 47 minutes.

1841–5, Ben Caunt

Bendigo returned from a trip to the USA and reclaimed his title. He and Caunt were matched for the championship in their third match. It was as savage as their previous two, with Caunt being disqualified in the 93rd round for going down without receiving a blow. A riot broke out. Caunt then retired from prize fighting. He died of pneumonia in 1861.

1845–50, William Thompson

Bendigo's next and final bout also ended in a disqualification. Against Tom Paddock he won when his opponent hit him while Bendigo had been knocked down and was still on the ground. He retired to become a well-known and fiery, if erratic, evangelistic preacher and the subject of an admiring poem by Sir Arthur Conan Doyle. A racehorse and a town in Australia were named after him. He died in 1880.

1850–1, William Perry

The 'Tipton Slasher' won and lost the championship on successive fouls. He claimed the title upon the retirement of Thompson after he had defeated Tom Paddock on a disqualification after 42 minutes of fighting in 1850. In his next contest he lost on a foul after 35 minutes to Harry Broome in Suffolk. Perry died in 1881.

1851–6, Harry Broome

Birmingham-born Broome did not push his luck. After he had won the title on a fortunate disqualification against Perry, he refused to give the former champion a return match, forfeited the title and returned to obscurity.

1856–8, Tom Paddock

A former farm worker, Paddock was such a brave fighter that by the time he won the championship he was almost worn out. Twice he defeated Aaron Jones, first in 121 rounds and then in 61 rounds. He lost a title bid against Bendigo. After winning the title from Broome he only had two more fights, losing to Tom Sayers and Sam Hurst. He died in 1863.

1858–60, Tom Sayers

Originally a bricklayer's mate, Sayers did not weigh more than 11 stone but he defeated William Perry giving away 2 stone and 5in in height. His greatest fight was against the American heavyweight John C. Heenan at Farnborough in 1860. Fighting with a badly damaged arm, Sayers lasted 42 rounds for a draw against his opponent before spectators broke into the ring and the match had to be abandoned. A testimonial to his courage raised £3,000 for the fighter. Sayers promptly retired. He died in 1865.

1860–1, Sam Hurst

Standing 6ft 3in in height, Hurst was known as the 'Stalybridge Infant'. He stopped former champion Tom Paddock in ten minutes for the title after Tom Sayers had retired, but lost it after a few months to Jem Mace.

1861–2, Jem Mace

Swaffham-born Mace provided the link between bare-knuckle fighting and the modern gloved game, straddling both eras. A student of the art of boxing, he toured all over the world with his boxing booth, taking on all-comers. A year after he first won the championship he lost his title temporarily to Tom King.

1862–3, Tom King

A former sailor, King lost to Jem Mace early in his career, but acquitted himself well, and in a return bout knocked out the champion in 21 rounds. He then defeated the formidable American John Heenan in 24 rounds at Wadhurst. He retired and became a successful bookmaker. He died in 1888.

1866–71, Jem Mace

After King's retirement, Mace regained the championship by stopping Joe Goss in 21 rounds. He then defeated the American champion Tom Allen in a bout for the world championship in Louisiana. Mace then retired and spent the rest of his life teaching boxing, promoting bouts and travelling with his booth.